Ei

JESUS' JOURNEY TO THE CROSS

I don't know of another pastoral writer in our age who speaks more aptly to our souls at any time of the year, but especially during the Lenten season and Easter, when we are eager to rethink the events in Jesus's life leading up to and including his crucifixion and resurrection. This book is replete with memorable stories and quotations that will refresh our hearts and equip us for living more spiritually day by day for the rest of our lives.

John Killinger,
former Professor of Preaching at Vanderbilt Divinity School,
past Senior Minister at First Congregational Church, Los Angles, CA,
and author of over 50 books.

William Tuck has done it again! Author of over 40 books, including *The Last Words from the Cross* and *The Church Under the Cross,* he continues his reflections on the centrality of the cross to the Christian faith. This time, instead of the seven last words, he focuses on six last deeds. The judgment of the crowd, the weeping of the women, Peter's denial and the rooster's crow, Pilate's handwashing, the pounding of the hammer, and finally Jesus' cry of accomplishment. It is a wonderful powerful statement of faith, challenging our response.

The Gospel begins with Jesus' proclamation, "The time is fulfilled, the Kingdom of God is at hand, repent and believe the Good News!" Instead of repentance and belief, he is confronted with rejection and opposition. His message is misunderstood. Working with the mind of a scholar and the heart of a pastor, William Tuck opens the Gospel story up for us, revealing and explaining Jesus' message in ways both moving and relevant for the readers. His writing is conversational and quite readable, both personal and practical and filled with applications and anecdotes. The book would be an excellent resource for a Lenten study for either a small group or individual use.

This is not a book to merely read through; it is intended to make a difference, to motivate and inspire, to make a difference in the life of the reader. Rev. Dr. Tuck confesses his purpose in writing this book, "My prayer is that we might respond and take up our cross and follow Christ today." I commend it to your attention.

Rev. Dr. David Moffett-Moore, Ph.D. D.Min
Academy of Parish Clergy, Fellow. Academy for Spiritual Formation, Forum Member, *The Jesus Manifesto* (on the Sermon on the Mount), *The Heart Cries Out* (on the Psalms)

Some stories are quite engaging but have a short shelf life. Some messages are compelling in a given moment, but when a more significant moment comes along, they are quickly forgotten. The Jesus story is not one of these stories, and the message of his journey to the cross is not one of these messages. This is a story and message that speaks to all circumstances, even the realities of a pandemic and a heightened awareness of racial inequalities which have overwhelmed all other concerns over the past few months.

Thus, William Powell Tuck's latest book *Jesus' Journey to the Cross* offers a timely resource not just for faith development but for social engagement in this critical time. In his customary, creative manner, Dr. Tuck examines this ancient story, which we often presume to know, and finds new insights. He takes a closer look at a series of scenes and characters and combining the knowledge of a scholar and the sensitivity of a pastor, identifies the probing questions each part of the story asks us.

From the crowd's fickle behavior, the women's weeping, and Peter's denial to Pilate's indecision, the nailing of Jesus to the cross, and Jesus' cry, "It is finished!" each scene speaks to matters of personal conscience and social concern – responsible decision making, things that should give rise to grief, the need to take responsibility, and the meaning of life and death. Thus, while this book will make a helpful devotional guide, especially during Lent, it deserves a larger place than that. As we are asking what Jesus would have us to do, with a bit more interest than usual, *Jesus' Journey to the Cross* offers insight, guidance, and provocation.

Chris Chapman,
Senior Pastor, First Baptist Church, Raleigh, N. C.

Lord, I Keep Getting a Busy Signal: Reaching for a Better Spiritual Connection
Overcoming Sermon Block: The Preacher's Workshop
A Revolutionary Gospel: Salvation in the Theology of Walter Rauschenbusch
Holidays, Holy Days, and Special Days
A Positive Word for Christian Lamenting: Funeral Homilies
The Forgotten Beatitude: Worshipping through Stewardship
Star Thrower: A Pastor's Handbook
A Pastoral Prophet: Sermons and Prayers of Wayne E. Oates (editor)
The Abiding Presence: Communion Meditations
Which Voice Will You Follow?
The Difficult Sayings of Jesus
Beginning and Ending a Pastorate
The Rebirth of the Church
Markers Along the Way: The Signs of Jesus in the Gospel of John

William Powell Tuck has served as both a parish pastor and a seminary professor. Bill, a native of Virginia, is a graduate of Bluefield College and the University of Richmond, Southeastern Baptist Theological Seminary and received his Th.D. degree from the New Orleans Baptist Theological Seminary. He has served Baptist congregations as Pastor and Interim Pastor in Virginia, Louisiana, Kentucky, and North Carolina, and was an adjunct professor at Virginia Intermont College, the University of North Carolina at Pembroke and at the Baptist Theological Seminary at Richmond, VA. He was also Professor of Preaching at the Southern Baptist Theological Seminary in Louisville, KY. He was awarded the Parish Pastor of the Year award by the Academy of Parish Clergy in 1997 and received an honorary Doctor of Divinity degree from the University of Richmond in 1977. The Boys & Girl's Club of America presented him The MEDALLION AWARD in 1999. In October of 2016 he received the Wayne Oates Award from the Oates Institute.

He is the author or editor of more than forty books, including *The Rebirth of the Church, Conversations with My Grandchildren, The Difficult Sayings of Jesus, Markers Along the Way, Star Thrower: A Pastor's Handbook, Modern Shapers of Baptist Thought in America, The Journey to the Undiscovered Country: What's Beyond Death?; Our Baptist Tradition; Holidays, Holy Days & Special Days,* and *The Church Under the Cross,* and is the author of more than 200 sermons and articles. He is married to Emily Campbell and is the father of two children and five grandchildren. He presently lives in Richmond, VA.

Website: www.friarsfragment.com

JESUS' JOURNEY TO THE CROSS

WILLIAM POWELL TUCK

For David,

Thank you for your leadership in guiding Bluefield College to become Bluefield University.

William P. Tuck

Energion Publications
Gonzalez, Florida
2021

ISBN: 978-1-63199-781-5
eISBN: 978-1-63199-782-2

Energion Publications
P. O. Box 841
Gonzalez, Florida 32560

energion.com

In Memory
of
my sister, June
my brother, Preston
and
my dear friend, Paul Simmons

TABLE OF CONTENTS

FOREWORD

Jesus' Journey to the Cross by William Powell Tuck is…

Straightforward.
Simple and Clear.
Direct.
Powerful.

These are words I would use to describe William Powell Tuck's latest book (of more than forty), *Jesus' Journey to the Cross*.

With clear Biblical exposition—helping us see and feel The Story as well as read it; and

With telling illustrations from daily life—linking our experiences with those of Jesus, his friends, and those who killed Him;

And with language of instant urgency—"Shouting," "Cries of Weeping," "Denial," "Pouring of Water," "Pounding of Hammer," "Cry of Triumph";

Dr. Tuck helps us walk with Jesus, from Pain to Glory.

His brief book inspires as it teaches, so that we, too, can Walk the Walk, we, too can find that place of Hope that says, "Because he lives, we too shall live."

Dr. J. Gordon Kingsley
12th President, William Jewell College
Principal Emeritus, Harlaxton College (England)

PREFACE

When Jesus began his ministry in Galilee, Mark tells us that he came proclaiming the good news about God, and he summarized Jesus' declaration in four dimensions: the time is fulfilled, the Kingdom of God is "at hand," repent, and believe the good news (Mark 1:14-15). The Kingdom of God was central in the teachings of Jesus, and most of his parables declared in their message what the Kingdom of God was like. Jesus' proclamation declared that God was a God of love not vindictive, compassionate not judgmental, forgiving not cruel, seeking us not rejecting us, redeeming us not condemning us, available not remote, sacrificial not demanding, and accepting not exclusive. If persons responded to this kingdom's message, there would be peace, love, justice, righteousness, brotherhood, and genuine redemption.

Unfortunately, the message of Jesus was challenged by the religious leaders of the day, and soon they sought a way to silence him and kill him. The disciples had hoped that Jesus was the Messiah, and this hope seemed to be realized when he entered Jerusalem and the crowd responded with cheers of excitement and acclamation. However, the Messiah they envisioned was a political figure who would overthrow the Roman rule and not one who would be crucified. A large portion of all the Gospels is filled with Jesus' journey to the cross. Shortly after the crowds' jubilation on Jesus' entrance to Jerusalem at the beginning of the Passover Feast, he is betrayed, arrested, brought before pseudo trials, including the Roman leaders, Herod, and Pilate, who ultimately delivered him before the crowd to be crucified. He was beaten severely, forced to bear his cross to Calvary as the women wept as he passed by, and then nailed to the cross by the Roman soldiers where he eventually died. I have sought to examine this sorrowful journey in the following pages and share my perspective on its meaning for us today. This is one person's attempt to understand the sad journey of Jesus and to discern the message the Gospel writers were seeking to unfold for their readers. But I send up a "caution flag" that Richard Rohr denotes: "It seems that we Christians have been worshiping Jesus' journey instead of doing his journey."[1] I believe the Gospel writers were expecting its readers not only to follow the story but respond to the call to follow the Christ who gave his life for us. My prayer is that we indeed might respond and take up our cross and follow Christ today. I want to express my appreciation to Rand Forder, a fellow minister, for his careful reading of my original manuscript.

1   Richard Rohr, *Everything Belongs: The Gift of Contemplative Prayer* (New York: A Crossroad Book, 2003). 20.

1.

THE SHOUTING
OF THE PEOPLE:

HOSANNA TO CRUCIFY HIM

Matthew 21:1-11

During most of his ministry, Jesus was surrounded by crowds. Crowds reached out to touch him that they might be healed. Crowds hung on his words hoping to understand something more about God. Crowds were amazed at his miracles. Their voices cried out to him for help. Crowds gathered around Jesus, following him, listened to him, and hoped that somehow this one who amazed them so much might be the Messiah. In the last week of Jesus' life, crowds played a very prominent part. Look at the crowd's reaction to Jesus.

THE PASSOVER FEAST IN JERUSALEM

During the Passover Feast in Jerusalem, the people from all over Israel came to celebrate this national feast. The Jewish historian, Josephus, estimated that almost three million people crowded the holy city. In some ways, the crowds were inspired by Jesus when he entered the city. He came into Jerusalem riding upon a donkey. Crowds threw down palm branches and their outer garments in his pathway. They shouted, "Hosanna to the one who comes in the name of the Lord." Through this prophetic picture or dramatic parable, Jesus attempted to teach the crowd a lesson about who he was. In ancient times a king, when he was going to war, would ride into battle on a horse. But when a king rode upon a donkey, it was a symbol of peace. In the day of Christ, a donkey was not looked upon as a contemptible or amusing animal. It was symbolic of peace. "He that comes," was a phrase depicting the Messiah. Jesus drew upon the ancient picture from Zechariah and other prophets which depicted the coming of the Messiah upon a lowly beast (Zechariah 9:9).

THE CROWDS REACTION TO JESUS

At Jesus' coming, the crowd shouted: "Hosanna." Too often we think that their hosanna meant praise to Jesus. But literally, the word "hosanna" meant "save us now." "Save us now," they yelled. "Here comes the King, the Messiah. Save us now." Fred Craddock believes that the "crowds represent the reappearance of the common people who had daily listened to Jesus in the temple.[1] The crowds were inspired by his presence and hoped that he might be the Messiah. But not all of this admiration turned to adoration. Later it would change to something else. "As Jesus, whose kingship is marked by a cross rather than a throne," Eugene Boring observes, "enters Jerusalem to these shouts of acclamation from those who

---

1   Fred B. Craddock, *Luke, Interpretation: A Bible Commentary for Teaching and Preaching* (Louisville: John Knox, 1990), 271.

later reject him, the deep irony in the opening scene in Jerusalem sets the tone for the passion story as a whole."[2]

At other times, the crowds were incited by Jesus. In just a few short days, after the cleansing of the Temple and the arrest of Jesus, the crowds, who had been inspired to shout, "Save us now," began to shout: "Crucify him, crucify him." How quickly their attitude changed, and they turned away from him. If you read the Scripture carefully, you will note that Jesus had received negative reactions from crowds before. Do you remember the response to the first sermon which Jesus preached in his hometown? They had expected a positive word from their hometown boy who had become famous. But his sermon shocked them, and they sought to stone him to death as they drove him out of the synagogue. The crowds in his own hometown turned against him.

On another occasion when Jesus had cast out the demons in the demoniac in the country of the Gadarenes, crowds tried to drive Jesus out of their country, because they were afraid of him. After one of his miracles, the crowds wanted to make Jesus a king. The crowd had not always responded positively to Jesus all along. Here the crowds are incited, "stirred up," according to the Scriptures by the chief priests.

Among the crowd in Jerusalem were the followers of Barabbas. Can you imagine their reaction when they heard that there could possibly be a choice between Jesus and Barabbas? At this word, all of the Barabbas supporters - the nationalists, who wanted to see the overthrow of the Roman government-packed into the courtyard. "Which one will you choose?" You can hear the crowd already shouting: "Give us Barabbas." I suspect that most of the people in this crowd were not the same people who were along the roadway shouting "Save us now," as Jesus rode by. This crowd thought that the end which they wanted to accomplish would come about by force not law. Their goal would be realized by violence-not by love, through war - not peace.

---

2   M. Eugene Boring, *The Gospel of Matthew, The New Interpreter's Bible* (Nashville: Abingdon Press, 1995), 404.

"Give us Barabbas," they cried. He symbolized for them the overthrow of the Roman government and the establishment again of the Jewish nation as a mighty military and political power. "Jesus doesn't represent that at all," they yelled, "Away with him." The popularity of Jesus was also beginning to wane, even with the common people, because they began to see that he was not the kind of Messiah that they had hoped for. His message gave another emphasis. He was different.

INCITING A CROWD

It is often easy, isn't it, for someone to incite the crowd and turn them in a certain direction? Crowds often seem to have a quasi-identity of their own. All you have to do is view films about Adolph Hitler to see how he was able to incite crowds in one of the most intelligent nations of the world and quickly turn those people away from justice, goodness, and the Christian perspective of life to a totally different way. He was able to enforce a law that required that the cross be removed in Christian churches and replaced by a swastika. Most of the churches obeyed this injunction. "There is no god," Hitler declared, "but Germany."

Crowds can be incited to do evil. Do you remember some of the awful things crowds did during the racial turmoil in this country? You could see the anger in the faces of persons filled with prejudice as black children and black adults were beaten, stoned, and driven out of towns. Study the faces of persons you see in the mob on television. Jim Jones incited a crowd and drew disciples around him. Later he convinced them to drink Kool-Aid which had been poisoned as a way of committing suicide. Powerful leaders can incite crowds, but they do not always achieve good ends. Isn't it strange that a person will often do something as a part of the crowd, the bunch, the gang, that he or she would never do alone? Sometimes individuals lose their sense of personal responsibility in a crowd. It disappears and a mob mentality takes over. Sometimes the crowd was stirred up against Jesus. They were incited by his presence. Jim Wallis, who has struggled nationally to combat many social evils, some incited by crowds, reminds us that "a political crisis could and should provoke a resurgence of faith and as far as we Christians and others are concerned, a moment and movement to reclaim Jesus."[3] We seek to confront the evil crowd with the principles of Jesus—love, justice, and righteousness.

Crowds can give us a false sense of security and courage. We can remain anonymous in a crowd. People change sometimes in a crowd. The crowd has been called the "12th" man on a football team. The home team crowd can often change the outcome of a game. Often the crowd becomes not just bad sports but "jerks." Several years ago, there was an article about the response of sports fans by James Nold, Jr. in the Scene of *The Courier-Journal* entitled "A Nation of Jerks"?

Steve Kerr was an outstanding guard for the University of Arizona basketball team. His father, who was president of the American University in Beirut, was assassinated by terrorists in 1984. In a 1988 Arizona - Arizona State game, ASU fans chanted: "PLO, PLO." "Go back to Beirut" and "Where's your dad?" when Kerr was introduced. It was justice that Kerr scored 22 points in a rout. But think what crude jerks the crowd were.[4]

A LOOK AT SAMUEL

Turn with me now from the roar of the crowd to a quiet time centuries ago. (1 Samuel 3:1-18) Many years ago, in a time much like our own, the word of God was rare and there were then, like now, no frequent visions of God. A young boy had gone to minister to an older priest named Eli whose eyesight was failing. That is probably the reason the boy slept close by him at night. He also stayed very close to the Ark of the Covenant, because one of his responsibilities was to keep the Eternal Flame burning near the

---

3   Jim Wallis, *Christ In Crisis: Why We Need to Reclaim Jesus* (New York: HarperCollins, 2019), 281.

4   James Nold, Jr., "A Nation of Jerks," *The Courier-Journal Scene* (March 14, 1992)

Ark. The voice of God was rare in those days. Although many Sunday-school quarterlies have depicted Samuel as a young child, the boy was more likely from fifteen to seventeen years old. He was a teenager, we would say. In this story, while Samuel was sleeping, he heard a voice in the night. As he had immediately done night after night, thinking that his master Eli was calling, he got up and went to see what needed tending. "I did not call," Eli says. He sends him back to his bed. But Samuel returns again and again, and finally, Eli realizes that maybe it is the voice of God that is speaking to Samuel. He then instructs the young lad to say, "Speak, Lord, for your servant hears."

The message of God is communicated to a young teenage boy about the judgment which God is sending upon this good man Eli and his family because the sons of Eli were scoundrels and they had corrupted the house of God and his service. The message was not easily received, and Samuel did not pass it on so quickly to Eli. But when Eli insisted, he shared the message with him. God's judgment did come, and this young boy rose to be one of the great prophets in the land of Israel.

SENSING THE VOICE OF GOD

In the Old Testament, the voice of God came to several other people at numerous times. Abraham sensed the voice of God calling him to go to a land that he knew not where. Moses, while he was on the back side of a mountain tending sheep, suddenly was confronted by a burning bush that was not consumed. And in that burning bush, he met the presence of God's spirit. Isaiah, went to the temple as was his custom, following the death of the great, beloved King of Israel, and he had a vision of God high and lifted up. Jeremiah, when he was a young lad tending his daily tasks, was confronted by the presence and power of God as he called him into his service. Ezekiel, by the bank of a river in a strange land, was confronted by the power and presence of God. Paul, traveling to persecute the Christians in Damascus, had a great light overshadow him, and he sensed the very power and presence of God, and he too responded to the voice.

JESUS HEARS THE VOICE OF GOD

It is interesting to recall that on some of the most significant times in the life of Jesus, he heard the voice of God. He heard the voice of God at his baptism, on the Mount of Transfiguration, and in the moments of his dying. But the Jewish teachers taught in the day of Jesus that the voice of God was no longer heard. They believed that God's voice came only indirectly to persons. But the scriptures tell us that Jesus heard God's voice directly on at least three occasions.

The temptation experience of Jesus was not likely a one-time occurrence, but it was probably a continuous struggle throughout his life. The temptation to turn stones into bread was the temptation to use "material" ends to win the people. The temptation to jump off the temple was the temptation to win people by magic or sensational means. The third temptation to worship Satan was the temptation to use the power of evil to reach people. Like you and me, Jesus struggled between the voice of God and the voice of evil in seeking to fulfill his ministry.

DOES THE VOICE OF GOD STILL COME?

We probably would not debate today that the voice of God has come. But does the voice of God still come? Can you and I today still hear God addressing us in some way? One of the reasons we sometimes have difficulty discerning what is the voice of God is that there are so many voices demanding our attention and calling to us saying: "I am the way of life." Many voices call to us saying: "Walk within my way and you will have abundant living." "Take my way and you will share in plenty." "Take my way and you will feel delightful and happy."

The Voice of Materialism

One of these voices today is the voice of materialism or consumerism. This voice tells us that we are what we possess. What we have makes us who and what we are. It says that we in essence are judged by the things we have. Too many of us too quickly and too foolishly fall into this kind of trap.

Eugene Ionesco, in a short play entitled *The New Tenant*, which was performed in Paris, tells about a man who was moving into his new apartment. The movers bring in a sofa, a table, a refrigerator, some chairs, kitchen furniture, and then they bring in two more sofas, and some more furniture. After a while, the movers open up the ceiling and begin to let furniture down through the ceiling. The room is completely filled up and piled high. Furniture has spilled over onto the sidewalk and into the River Seine. There is no more room, and a voice asks: "Is there anything else we can do?" A voice from beneath the pile of furniture replies: "The light. Get the lights." "Right," the voice responds. And the light is turned off and the play comes to an end. What is the message? We are encumbered by our possessions. Our possessions possess us. Do not buy into the philosophy of life that tells you loudly and clearly that material things are the essence of what constitutes authentic living.

The "Playboy" Voice

A second voice that we often succumb to is the voice that has sounded loudly and clearly for decades. And that voice is the playboy philosophy of life. This philosophy says that free sex is what constitutes authentic living. This approach believes that one lives for instant gratification. This attitude has no high regard for another person. Persons are treated as things or as objects. Others are seen as objects to gratify your sexuality. Others are there for your pleasure. No lasting commitments are made. Women are depicted as a plaything for men, a bunny. Sex is for the moment and no lasting relationships are established. They do not talk about marriage, because sex is merely for one's own gratification. A similar philosophy is sold to us by those who live for adrenaline-filled sports, gambling, and drug use.

This philosophy is sold to us through music, television, movies, books, and magazines. Many in our society have swallowed it hook, line, and sinker. Do not buy into this philosophy, because it is a dead-end street that will haunt us again and again with guilt and tragedy. The movies do not usually depict the outcome, the discards, and the rejects that come from that kind of life. The Church needs to challenge that philosophy clearly for the cheap approach to life that it is.

THE VOICE OF CHEAP AND CIVIL RELIGION

Third, do not listen to the voice that is calling us to cheap religion and civil religion. There are many voices in our land today which are telling us that religion is primarily something that we use to make us feel good, or that real religion is a "prosperity Gospel". Religion is a spectator's sport for many. If we are entertained, then we feel religious. When we get goose bumps, this approach affirms that this makes me right with God. An even more distorted view is the one that equates "whatever my country wants" with what is the essence of religion. And so, we wrap God and country in the same flag and bow down and worship both country and God at the same shrine, and we never see that this is idolatry. Many who advocate this kind of philosophy of life, call themselves very moral, yet they do not recall the judgment that comes from the Old Testament prophets who thundered the warning that God is above country. We can never equate what one country does, no matter how good it is, as God's way. We cannot equate God and country, religion, and the flag. Do not buy into cheap religion that offers us salvation without commitment, grace without surrender, and redemption without sacrifice. Jesus calls us to take up our cross and follow him.

THE VOICE OF SELFISHNESS

Fourth, do not follow that voice ringing within our ears telling us that the basic philosophy of life is "meism." Selfishness is the main concern of this approach. Whatever I want is the only judgment upon anybody else's importance. Every other person in life is important to me, in this philosophy, as he or she does something for me. They are pawns on my table in what they can give and do to satisfy me. My world is surrounded by me. People are important in what they can do for my values, my standards, my promotions. The "meism" philosophy circulates all around us today as many constantly look out only for number one.

A story is told of the esteemed Japanese Christian leader, Toyohiko Kagawa, arising out of an American speaking tour. Dr. Kagawa had written many books, had been a notable church leader, and had received international recognition as a Christian spokesperson. On one occasion, he had been scheduled to address a large convention of clergy and lay leaders. Before the service, he and the denominational officials who were to escort him to the platform stopped in the restroom. As often happens at a large convention, many of the men who had been in the restroom that day had missed the trashcan with their paper towels. When Dr. Kagawa's escorts left the restroom for the platform, they assumed he was right behind them. When they reached the platform, however, he was nowhere in sight. Returning to the restroom, they found Dr. Kagawa carefully picking up all the papers that others had left for the janitor.

Too many feel that they can throw anything they want on the ground, or say whatever they want, without regard for others. Others exist only to meet their needs or to fulfill their ends.

LISTEN FOR THE VOICE OF GOD

Many voices are crying to us in our land calling us to a lower way. But the voice of God is seeking to penetrate our very being, and we need to listen for it. Listen. It may be a still, small voice that comes echoing softly through the roaring noise of the other voices. But listen and see if you can hear it.

Speak Clearly

First, I believe that this voice will whisper to you one thing for sure and say: "Learn to speak clearly and distinctly." In an age of so much "gobbledygook" and double talk, do we not need to speak more plainly about the things of God and life? Do we not need people in politics and religion who will stand up clearly for what they believe? We can see then what their stand really is, and we will either like it or not like it. We will either follow them or not follow them. I hope that all people will learn to speak plainly and distinctly in an age that avoids clear speech.

The Pentagon, which is not often noted for clear talk, put up a sign once which read: "This passageway is non-conducive for an indefinite period of time to traffic." What that sign meant was, "Keep out!" Why not just say it plainly and clearly?

Communication is a difficult problem in our society. We often feel that communication is not clear from our politicians, teachers, preachers, and others. We long for better communication between husband and wife, parents, and children. In an age of noise and confusion, we long for a clear distinct word.

In my "student" church in Virginia, there was a farmer who was the one to whom the church would turn when they wanted a clear word. If they needed insight into a matter, someone would ask, "Joe, what do you think?" They knew his word could be trusted. He always spoke clearly, without an agenda. He and his word could be trusted.

Jesus Christ is the epitome of one who learned to speak clearly. They didn't crucify Jesus because they couldn't understand what he was saying. They understood very clearly what he was saying. The religious leaders knew that he was challenging their religion and their way of life. He was calling them to a higher way. The call to speak simply does not mean that you speak tritely. Deep meaning can be expressed simply without being trite. For something to be simple does not mean that it has to be simplistic. We need to learn to make the distinction between the two and learn to speak plainly and simply so people can hear us.

An Accepting Voice

Second, I hope that you will also hear the voice that comes to you saying to you that you are loved and acceptable to God. You notice in the New Testament that Jesus told us that God comes searching after us even while we are sinners. We do not become sanctified, and then we become OK to God. God loves us even while we are sinful, and God comes seeking and searching after us to bring us back to himself. Now that doesn't mean that God loves our sin. But God loves us as individuals and calls us to the very highest and best we can be with our own gifts.

I read recently of a hospital chaplain who said that at last, he had gotten to the point where he could look into the mirror and say, "I like you." A lot of us don't like ourselves very much. We are too tall, too short, too thin, or too heavy. We don't like this or that about ourselves. We have to learn to accept ourselves, and as Paul Tillich says, "accept God's acceptance of us." We are loved by God, and God cared for us so much that He came into the world to die for us. Hear the voice of God that comes to you and says to you, "I appreciate you; I love you, and I want to guide you in life."

A Voice of Integrity

Third, listen also for the voice of God that comes saying to us that God is a God of integrity, and God wants us to have high values in the way we live and walk. It is sad today to live in a world in which the trust level has fallen so low. We have seen this loss from cheating in middle school to corruption in government. We have gotten to the point that we really do not know how much we can trust a commercial on television or how much we can trust an advertisement in the paper. Some of our "so-called" television news stations and "social media" platforms are suspect, too. Too often these ads do not live up to what they say they can do or will do. We find young people who participate in shoplifting or cheat in school. I heard about books that were stolen from a seminary library. The seminary had to put in a new system to protect the books. What has happened to our value system in our world today? Where is integrity? Where are the people who stand up for those things that are worthwhile, lasting, and meaningful? When is a person's word his or her bond? What has happened to our real sense of integrity and values? We need to hear God calling us to live a life of honesty, decency, and fairness in the way we relate to others.

General William Dean was taken prisoner in the Korean War. He thought he was going to die. He had been in prison for three years and before his capture had survived in the mountains for thirty-five days with little food. He wrote his family a letter thinking that it would be the last he would ever write to them, and he said something like this: "Mildred, I want to thank you for the twenty-four wonderful years that we shared together and I love you." To his daughter, June, he encouraged her not to delay making her mother a grandmother. Then he wrote directly to his young son, Bill. "Bill, remember that integrity is the most important thing of all. Let that always be your aim. "Let us listen to the voice of integrity that calls us to a higher level than we have ever realized. Our call is not to give way to the lesser and base values in life.

A Voice of Discipline

Fourth, I hope that we will also listen to the voice that is calling us to a sense of discipline. Young Samuel had disciplined his life to respond to the call of his master. Discipline is an unpopular word today. So many people want freedom. They don't want any restraints or demands. They want absolute, total freedom. But absolute total freedom only brings anarchy. Those in life who have found the most lasting values have been those who have been able to discipline themselves. No one can ever really become a musician without discipline. Nobody ever becomes a good athlete without discipline. Nobody becomes a medical doctor, attorney, dentist, etc., without some kind of discipline in his or her life.

We had a young man in a church where I was a pastor who broke the state record in track for Virginia when he was in high school. He didn't get up one day and say, "You know, I think I want to be a great runner," and so broke the record that day. He got up day after day, week after week, year after year, and ran fifteen miles a day. He disciplined his body and mind to do that. No, he didn't start running fifteen miles the first day, of course. He built up to that. He ran and ran until he became one of the greatest cross-country runners in the state. It came about because of discipline.

Jesus has told us that His way is narrow. The broad way that leads to destruction is the way without any kind of control, without any kind of restraints. But Christ calls us to a narrow way that demands discipline. But his way is always narrow. Love is narrow. It focuses on particular persons. When I read something, that means that I have narrowed my vision to that book or magazine. When I choose a vocation, I narrow it to that one. There needs to be some sense of discipline and control in one's life or we become totally chaotic without direction and meaning. I hope we can hear the voice of God calling us to discipline.

A Challenging Voice

Fifth, like young Samuel, I hope we also can hear the voice of God as it calls us to a new challenge that lies before us. Samuel responded to God and met the challenge before him. We should never be content with where we are spiritually.

Around the turn of the 20th century, the director of the U.S. Patent office resigned. He said that all the great inventions had already been discovered. He thought that there would no longer be a need for his office. And this was around the turn of the century. Look at the inventions which have been discovered since then.

Young people, the greatest books, the greatest music, the greatest discoveries have not yet been realized. Just look at what has happened in the last few years with computers, smartphones, iPad, zoom, and the internet. The greatest dreams of what is going to be accomplished in space, in the ocean, in the environment, in medicine, in science, in technology, etc., are still waiting to be discovered.

There is a great, bold, exciting adventure lying before us, and I hope that you and I will not buy into the voice that says everything has already been done and accomplished. There is much left for us to do because the greatest challenge is still ahead. In the areas of war, poverty, disease, and human relations, there are areas that challenge us. This is true in the scientific and literary fields as well. Many new worlds loom before us. Why do we settle for the present when the pull of the future is upon us? The greatest challenges still lie ahead, and I hope, young people and adults, that like Samuel, when we hear the voice of God, we will accept our responsibility and say, "Speak, Lord, for your servant hears." Respond like Samuel and let's do our task.

A number of years ago a football team was being absolutely stomped by its opponent. The score was fifty-eight to nothing, and they were in the last quarter. The team that was losing had been beaten in every way by the stronger team. The coach put in a new tailback who was not battered. The quarterback received the ball, and then turned around and tried to give it to this player. He was chasing him in the backfield and trying to pass him the ball. The coach kept yelling from the sideline: "Give the ball to Callahan. Give the ball to Callahan." The quarterback finally hollered back and said, "But Callahan says he don't want the ball."

We are in a world in which there are a lot of problems and a lot of challenges. I hope that we will not be like the young tailback and say, "I don't want the ball." The ball is now being passed into our hands. You and I have responsibilities to do something about them and do our part in seeking to help overcome the problems in the world today. You and I need to rise up to meet the challenges that are there. The ball is in our court, and we are challenged now not just to be recipients, not to receive what others have done for us, but now we are challenged to be a part of the force that will make a difference in society as we seek to overcome and change some of the things in our world.

LISTEN FOR THE VOICE OF CHRIST

There are many voices calling to us from all kinds of quarters today saying "walk in my path." I hope that you will listen and determine that the true voice amid all the false voices is the voice that calls you and me to the highest and best we can be. I hope that you and I will never settle for the commonplace or the mediocre but will hear the voice calling us to be more than we are. I hope that you and I will hear the voice of God which is calling us to discipline our life and give it control and direction. I hope that you and I will hear the voice of God in the midst of all the confusion, corruption, crime, sin, lying, and cheating which says to us to stand up for integrity and decency. Let our word be a word that stands for truth and high values. I hope that you will hear the voice of God, echoing among all the voices around you, which says that you are loved and accepted. This voice of God declares that you can be forgiven and that you can rise up as a new person to be God's son or daughter to live for God in the world. Amid all the loud confusing voices, I hope that you can hear the whisper of the still, small voice of God calling you to come, follow him. The Christlike way is the only real abundant life. I hope you will not miss it because you have chosen the broad way instead of the narrow way. Listen. Listen. God is speaking. Let us hear God's voice and follow.

O Loving God, we confess that so often we are confused by the sounds around us. We give in to the lesser voices that call out our low selves. May we learn to hear your voice among all the false voices and rise to the higher values, the better ways, the Christlike way. Amen.

2

THE CRIES OF WEEPING:

THE TEARS OF WOMEN

Luke 23:26-31

Let me picture the setting of our text. Jesus had already been arrested. He had gone through a mock trial; he had been convicted, scourged, and beaten by the soldiers. Then they placed a heavy wooden cross upon his shoulders. As the custom was in that day, Jesus had to bear that cross down the most public thoroughfare and the longest route to where he would be crucified. This was a visible sign to the people watching that the criminal, who was bearing that cross, was being dreadfully punished. A soldier would walk before the person bearing the cross with a placard announcing the individual's crime. This was a warning by the Roman government to anyone who would try to do anything similar.

Jesus, having already been beaten severely, carried the cross for some distance and then collapsed under the weight of the heavy load. A Roman soldier reached over with the flat side of his spear and tapped on the shoulder a visitor to the city, named Simon of Cyrene. He was compelled to help bear that cross to the place where Jesus would be crucified. As Jesus slowly moved along the road to Golgotha, he heard the loud cries of women who were pouring forth their grief and lamentations at what they were witnessing. Luke alone shares this episode in Jesus' journey to the cross. The gospel writers note that Jesus always seemed to be surrounded not only by men but by women as well. It is interesting to observe that there is no report of any women opposing Jesus.

WOMEN'S SUPPORT FOR JESUS

Women supported Jesus during the difficult times of his ministry as well as during the joyful occasions. Women remained faithful when he was persecuted as they had been faithful during the times when he was praised. Women were among Jesus' followers at the wedding feast at Cana. Mary and Martha opened their house to him at Bethany. These two women were at Lazarus' tomb. A woman had anointed Jesus' feet when he ate a meal in the home of Simon. Jesus had praised a widow at the temple for her sacrificial offering. Women were at the cross when the men had fled. And a woman named Mary, who stood weeping at Jesus' tomb, was the first person to see the risen Lord. Women remained faithful to Jesus throughout his ministry.

Here on this thoroughfare to death, women were present again, but this time they were weeping bitterly, wailing in their laments at what they saw happening to Jesus. But as Jesus heard them, he said a strange thing to the women, "Daughters of Jerusalem, do not weep for me." Why did Jesus rebuke them? Why does he tell them not to weep for him? He seemed unwilling to accept their sympathy at this time when the women felt such anguish for what they saw happening to him. He had accepted kindness at other times when people had extended it to him. He had accepted the kindness only a week before from a woman who washed his feet and poured a flask of costly ointment upon him as she bathed his feet with her tears. He had often accepted the gift of kindness and hospitality at the home of Mary and Martha and others. But on this road to his death, he rebuked these women and seemed unwilling to accept their expression of sympathy.

WAS THE WEEPING REAL?

Do you suppose that Jesus questioned whether this public display of weeping was genuine? In that day, women were often professional mourners who would parade through the village streets and make a public display of grief with loud lamentations. Jesus may have felt that *their display of grief was not real* and so he rebuked them. Jesus always despised shams. He wanted a response from those who were genuinely sad at what was happening to him.

Jesus may have rebuked the women because he knew that secretly *they feared for themselves* much more than for him. His approaching death was a sign to them of what might happen to all of them one day from the Roman government if their families did not follow strictly the mandate of Rome. Jesus had wept over Jerusalem before (Luke 19:41-44), and here he is *warning them of the coming destruction of Jerusalem* and the weeping the women will have then. Alan Culpepper believes this lament over the suffering to come is an important element in Luke's passion narrative. "Here is a moving aspect of the meaning of Jesus' death. He had called for repentance and wept over the city," Culpepper writes. "When his pleas were not heeded, however, he joined himself to the plight of those who suffer the ravages of violence, dying with criminals on a cross."[1] Justo Gonzalez believes the words of the women may have at least two meanings. They may proclaim the destruction of Jerusalem that will come forty years later, but also might be an "eschatological warning" of the evil to come upon the world.[2]

---

1   R. Alan Culpepper, *The Gospel of Luke, The New Interpreter's Bible,* IX (Nashville: Abingdon Press, 1995), 453.

2   Justo L. Gonzalez, *Luke, Belief: A Theological Commentary on the Bible* (Louisville: Westminster John Knox Press, 2010), 262.

Maybe they were also weeping from their *own sense of guilt*. Just a week before some of these same women may have been a part of the crowd of people who yelled "Hosanna" when Jesus entered Jerusalem and later, they quickly changed their cry to "Crucify him." Now they realized that the Roman soldiers really were going to crucify Jesus and they may have been weeping out of a sense of guilt.

In one of Alan Paton's moving novels, *Cry, the Beloved Country*, a black African minister, Steven Kumalo, has just visited his son in prison who has been arrested for murder. An anguished cry rises from Kumalo's lips as he speaks with a fellow minister.

> He is a stranger ... I cannot touch him; I cannot reach him. I see no shame in him, no pity for those he has hurt. Tears come out of his eyes, but it seems he weeps only for himself, not for his wickedness, but for his danger.

The man cried out, "Can a person lose all sense of evil? A boy brought up as he was brought up? I see only his pity for himself, he who has made two children fatherless."[3]

Did Jesus see in the faces and cries of these women only guilt and pity for themselves? It is hard to know. Maybe Jesus saw the weeping of the women as *a sign of sentimentality or emotionalism*. There was no one who hated pretense and sham more than Jesus. He knew the folly of trusting in emotionalism. The women may have been touched emotionally by the pain and suffering of Jesus but there was no real depth of concern. They had moved so quickly and easily from "Hosanna" to "Crucify him." Emotions can change with the wind. We have all seen certain preachers or lay persons who could turn on a "faucet" of tears at a needed moment in a speech. These are often tears drawn from the play actor's skill and not from the depths of one's being. Jesus knew that no momentary tears would suffice for his pain. He, likewise, does not want merely seasonal tears at Lent from us. He will not be satisfied with potted

---

3   Alan Paton, *Cry, The Beloved Country*, (New York: Charles Scribner's Sons, 1948), 109

lilies as a memorial to him to atone for our guilt or be satisfied with a short fast. He longs for something more.

HOW COULD THEY NOT WEEP?

"Weep not," Jesus said. But how could these women not weep? These women and men had put so much hope in Jesus. They thought that he might possibly be the Messiah, the promised one of God, come to set them free from their bondage to Rome. Now look at him. He was bearing a cross; his back was cut and bleeding from the whipping by the Roman soldiers. A crown of thorns was pressed tightly around his brow. He was stumbling in the street under the weight of his cross, eating the dust of the street, and hearing the curses and ridicule from the soldiers and likely from many in the crowd of people along the sides of the street as well. It was hard for the people to see Jesus treated this way for they had seen his miracles. He had healed the sick, given sight to the blind, hearing to the deaf, made the lame walk and lepers clean. He had even raised the dead. He had reached out to the untouchables in society, not only the lepers, but publicans, prostitutes, slaves, sinners, and other outcasts of society. He had been a friend to the poor, women, and children as well as the needy. He had taught them that God's kingdom was at hand and had boldly challenged the religious leaders. Why should they not weep? All their hopes seemed to be dashed to the ground as this young carpenter was led to a cross. The man they believed was the promised one from God was being led away to be crucified. Why not weep? What else could they do?

IS THERE NO PLACE FOR WEEPING?

Weep not. Was Jesus telling us that there was no place for crying? Could it possibly be true that our Lord was saying, "Do not weep"? Surely, surely that is not true. Listen to the cry of the Psalmists:

> Like a bird alone in the desert
> or an owl in a ruined house

I lie awake and I groan,
like a sparrow lost on a roof.
Ashes are the bread that I eat,
  I mingle tears with my drink.

Psalm 102

 From the depths I cry to you, O Lord, give heed to my lament.

Psalm 130

Listen to the words from the Book of Lamentations 2:18:

"Let tears run down like a river day and night…Give thyself
no rest; let not the apple of thine eye cease."

No, I do not believe that Jesus is telling us that we should never
cry. Jeremiah had poured forth rivers of tears. King David wept for
his dead son. Even Jesus had wept beside the grave of his friend
Lazarus. The apostle Paul and countless others poured forth tears
in times of grief or contrition. They longed like the Psalmist that
"they that sow tears shall reap in joy," (Psalm 126:5).

SOME HAVE AN ANATHEMA FOR GRIEVING

Our society doesn't want to give much place for tears today.
There seems to be a taboo on any external sign of emotions. People
expect mourners to get over their grief quickly. When a person ex-
presses grief by crying openly, people seem to be disturbed by that
person's tears. Tears are often seen as a sign of weakness or they are
seen as a demeaning characteristic. A few years ago, when one of
our political candidates cried in public, reporters and the public
scorned him so much that he eventually dropped out of the political campaign. As a candidate, he was viewed as being too weak to
hold public office. All because he wept publicly. No, society does
not want to give much place for tears today. Kate Bowler relates in
her book, *Everything Happens for a Reason,* the many pseudo reasons

many persons gave her about her suffering with cancer and their unwillingness to allow her to question or grieve over her condition.[4]

Many of our modern funeral homes have perpetuated this taboo attitude regarding any emotional expression of grief by placing the mourners behind a screen or in a private room off to the side of the chapel. This infers that there is something bad or unacceptable about public expressions of grief. "Tears," said Voltaire, "are the silent language of grief."

Modern society likes to ridicule the old-fashioned wakes and ancient customs of burial and mourning rites. Their functions, which often served as a real outlet for experiences of grief, have now been replaced with sleeping pills, tranquilizers, stimulants, alcohol, or other evasive means of escaping the reality of what has really happened. Our denial of weeping is a poisonous infection in the bloodstream of life. Tears have been called "the safety valves of the heart" when too much pressure is laid on it. I wonder if the young mother who said that she was complimented for acting like a zombie at the death of her child would have taken her own life if her friends had permitted her the normal release of her emotions instead of praising her for such unnatural behavior.

John Sutherland Bonnell refers to a young doctor and his wife who came to talk with him about some marital problems. "There is something wrong with our marriage and there always has been," said the doctor. "I love my wife very dearly and I hope she loves me, but there seems to be some barrier in her life that keeps her from entering wholeheartedly into our marriage. She seems to build up a wall against me. Our marriage has never been really happy either physically or spiritually. I am hoping that there is something you can tell us that will help to change this situation." The young wife broke down, weeping, and said: "I know I don't love my husband as I ought to. I try to but something holds me back."

After five or six interviews, Dr. Bonnell noted that the wife recalled many memories from her childhood, and they were all

---

4   Kate Bowler, *Everything Happens for a Reason* (New York: Random House, 2018).

closely associated with her father. She had been very close to her father, the apple of his eye. He often played with her, and she would sit for long periods on his lap. When the doctor's wife was only eight years old, and while she was away visiting a relative, her father suddenly died, and they did not bring her home until after the funeral. Without the presence of her father the child was completely lost and brokenhearted, and, although they told her that he had died, she had not experienced death in any way and the word was meaningless to her. She felt repulsed and rejected by her mother and later by her stepfather who only tolerated her. Throughout her teenage and college years and even into her period of engagement, marriage, and birth of her children, she continued to sustain a mental image of her father as though he were still living and that somewhere she would one day find him again.

Dr. Bonnell observed: "She couldn't give herself completely to her husband because her father was still her first love. She felt that loyalty and devotion to him demanded that everybody else in her life would have a secondary place. This fact she would have to see and understand for herself; not only had she failed to grasp it intellectually, but it had to penetrate her feelings. She had to know in her deepest being that her father had died and that in her lifetime she would never see him again."

Dr. Bonnell then talked to the young woman about death and unresolved grief. Later he received a call from her very disturbed husband: "What is happening with my wife?" he asked. "For two nights in succession, she has cried almost all night long, sobbing till her whole body is shaking. I am very much alarmed. Has something gone wrong in the counseling?" Dr. Bonnell assured him that nothing was wrong but that this was the belated grief of his wife on behalf of her father and to let her continue until her weeping ended on its own. After several more interviews with Dr. Bonnell, the young wife learned to transfer her affection from her dead father to her husband. "Our marriage now," the doctor called later to say, "is filled with a happiness that we have never known before. It is as though we are on our honeymoon. We have a joy and happiness in each other that is beyond measure."[5]

CRYING: A NORMAL RESPONSE

Why should anyone feel ashamed of crying in the face of sorrow? Tears are the avenue of expression which God has given to us to release the pent-up emotions which, if unresolved, may distort our very personality with the power of their internal agitation. "There is a sacredness in tears," Washington Irving once penned. "They are not the mark of weakness but of power. They speak more eloquently than ten thousand tongues. They are the messengers of overwhelming grief, of deep contrition, and of unspeakable love." Another voice, that of the poet Leigh Hunt, expressed it this way: "God made both tears and laughter, and both for kind purposes; for as laughter enables mirth and surprise to breathe freely, so tears enable sorrow to vent itself patiently."

There are times we need to weep. Do it with understanding, compassion, and acceptance. Some claim the only verse from the New Testament they can quote is "Jesus wept." Remember it and weep with the knowledge that Jesus said: "Blessed are they that mourn; for they shall be comforted" (Matthew 5:4, KJV).

A SUMMONS TO COMMITMENT

When Jesus was telling these women, "Do not weep," he was not giving a universal declaration about crying. Go further into the text. "Do not weep for me," Jesus said. Our Lord seemed to be saying: "I do not want your pity; I do not want your pity because I am within God's will." The gospel writers now saw him as the "Suffering Servant." Jesus did not see himself as a victim but as a victor. He didn't want sympathy; he wanted sacrifice. He did not want pity; he wanted commitment from people. He would not settle for cheap grace but called his disciples to take up their cross

---

5   John Sutherland Bonnell, *No Escape from Life*, (New York: Harper & Row, 1958), 61-64.

and follow him. He was going to drink the cup of suffering, and he challenged others to share that cup with him.

In the ancient catacombs, a picture of a lamb was discovered. In the early symbol of Jesus, the lamb was wearing a crown on his head, and under the crook of its forearm is a scepter. Here is a picture of the Lamb that was slain — a conquering, victorious Lamb. Jesus did not want pity from others. He wanted them to see that he was coming as God's victorious servant. "Do not weep for me," Jesus declared. "In the world you have tribulation. But be of good cheer, I have overcome the world."

"Weep not for me", Jesus says, "but weep for yourself." Weep for yourself. Jesus warns his listeners about an impending judgment. His words are prophetic. There will come a time in your own history, (and it happened just a few years later, 66 to 70 AD), when Israel rose up in rebellion against the Roman Government, but they were defeated. The temple was destroyed, and their holy city Jerusalem lay in ruins, and thousands were killed. The reference to the proverb about the green and dry branches sounds strange to us today. Jesus was noting that if he who was innocent was suffering for something he had not done, think what it was going to be like when the nation actually rebelled against the government. Although it was usually seen as a great tragedy for a Jewish woman not to have a child, Jesus predicted that during the days of terror before them, childless women would thank God that they had no sons or daughters to be murdered by the government.

WEEP FOR YOURSELVES

"Weep for yourselves," Jesus says. Weep for yourselves. Weep for your selfishness; weep for your egotism. Weep for your sins. Weep for the fact that God's moment of salvation came, and you rejected it and did not receive God's salvation. Weep for yourselves. Let there be tears of repentance because of missed opportunity. Each of us bears responsibility for our own sins. We can also weep for the sins of our society and nation. We can weep for injustice, racism, war, the climate crisis, world poverty, and many other communal sins.

Michael Quoist in a prayer poem has expressed that truth.

> To pity your sufferings and the sufferings of the world
> I manage very well, Lord
> But to weep for my own sins, that's another matter.
> I'd as lief bemoan those of others,
> It's easier. …
> I've found plenty of guilt …
> in many others, Lord, many others.
> All in all, in just about the whole world save me.[6]

AN APPROPRIATE WEEPING

It is easy to see the sins in others, but we must weep for our own sins. Nevertheless, there is a proper weeping. It is to identify with why Jesus wept. When Jesus came within sight of Jerusalem and looked upon the city, he said: "If only you had known, on this great day, the way that leads to peace! But no; it is hidden from your sight … you did not recognize God's moment when it came." Then he wept for the city. There is proper weeping and that is to weep as Jesus wept. Like our Lord, we weep because we realize that all of those Jesus wanted to reach with the message of God's love will not be reached. Weep for those who reject the kingdom of God and for those who turn away from God's promised One. Weep because all will not be converted. Weep for those who give in to selfishness, egotism, and greed.

Jesus has said there is a proper weeping. Weep for those who are willing to settle for cheap grace instead of God's costly love. Weep for those who want pseudo-religion instead of authentic religion. Weep for those who will settle for the artificiality of religion instead of genuine faith commitment. Weep for those who have taken holy things and profaned them. Weep for those who have taken the gospel of good news and made it trivial and trite.

---

6   Michel Quoist, *Prayers* (New York: Avon Books, 1975), 166.

Weep for those who have turned the church that God established to bring in his kingdom into a social and political club. Weep for politicians who have lost their integrity. Weep for the black people who suffer under apartheid in South Africa. Weep for the poor, the hungry, and the oppressed people of the world. Weep for the victims of injustice in our world. Weep for those who suffer from AIDS or are the victims of sexual abuse. Weep for those who are victims of discrimination and oppression.

Yes, there is a proper weeping. Weep for those who are victims of terrorists in places like Buenos Aires where the Israeli Embassy was destroyed. Weep for the terrorists who see killing as a just act. Weep for those who see no meaning in life and are depressed and lonely. Weep for those in the Near East who cannot live together. Weep for the economy of the former Soviet Union. Weep for our own economy. Weep for those who have no jobs. Weep for those who suffered from the coronavirus. Weep for those who are insecure. Weep for those who have pain and are suffering. Weep for our environment which we continue to pollute. Weep for our rivers, air, oceans, land, and our bodies. Weep that we don't care. Weep for those who claim to be Christians and never live the Christlike life. Weep for our churches that will settle for such shallow faith. Weep for those who "demand" much from God and give God almost nothing in service. Weep for yourself and your sins. Weep for those who crucify the Son of God. Weep for ourselves as we crucify him again. Weep that we are so far from loving or serving God as we should. Weep ... weep.

The Book of Revelation reveals a great promise for us. Listen to our hope.

We have seen a great mystery:
We shall all be changed.
We shall be raised in Christ
   as we were buried in Christ.
Death is swallowed up in victory.
The dwelling of God will be with his people,
   and death shall be no more.

There shall be no mourning, no crying nor pain;
sorrow and sighing shall flee away.
For the old things are disappearing.

(Revelation 21)

That is a wonderful, marvelous promise, but it has not yet been realized. We join our Lord in drinking the Cup of Sorrow if we are his true disciples. Our tears have not yet been wiped away. Why? We are a part of humanity, and as a part of humanity, there is still grief; there is still sorrow; there is still the need for repentance. There is still the need for confession. There is still pain and burdens. So, we lift our hearts to join with our Lord that we might feel his love for us today. Yes, there are times that we weep for ourselves, and times when we weep for others. In all our weeping we long to sense the healing grace of God. So, in the Lenten season, let us learn to weep again for the right reason. And weep we should.

Oh God, who has suffered for us in Christ Jesus, and whose heart aches because our hearts ache help us to sense your love for us. Help us to know that when we weep, you hear us and draw us close to your heart. Oh God, give us the courage to weep for the sins we have committed. When we weep as we bear the heavy burdens of life, help us to feel the sustaining grace of your strong hand upon us. We pray in the name of the one who knew pain and wept as we weep, even Jesus Christ, our brother and Lord. Amen.

3.

THE CROWING OF THE ROOSTER:

PETER'S DENIAL

Luke 22:54-61

As the high school students were walking down the hall at school, one of them turned to her friend, as she pointed to a star player on the basketball team, and said: "He's so cocky, isn't he?" Sometimes a person who is conceited or arrogant is described this way or in words like "cocksure" or "cock of the walk". Simon Peter might have been described this way. The rooster is an image that has been identified with Peter and his sense of self-assurance and later his denial of our Lord. Let's look at our text and set the stage for our thoughts today.

Simon Peter thought that the cause of Jesus was finished. His hopes and dreams about the Kingdom of God had been shattered by the arrest of Jesus. Now he stood in the courtyard below the palace of the High Priest, Caiaphas, and wondered what would happen to Jesus. His heart beat rapidly with fear. His spirit was frozen with terror. He was cold, weary from sleeplessness, frustrated, frightened, and did not know what to do. He moved closer in the crowd of people who were gathered in the courtyard to see the Nazarene. He walked cautiously to a brazier to warm himself from the coldness of the night air. Evidently, he had spoken to some of the people in the group around the fire, because they recognized his accent.

One turned to him and asked: "Are you not one of this Galilean's followers?" Peter pleaded ignorance. "I don't know what you are talking about." But the maid servant pressed further. "You are one of his disciples, aren't you? Your speech betrays you." He could not hide the fact that he was from Galilee. The Galilean accent was a thick, heavy burr. He could not deny it. In fact, the accent of the Galilean was considered to be so crude by some Jews that a Galilean was never asked to pronounce the benediction in the synagogue. "You are one of his disciples," the woman exclaimed again. This time Peter cursed and denied that he knew Jesus. Just as he denied Jesus the cockcrow sounded and he looked up, as Luke's gospel records, and he saw Jesus standing on the balcony above. Their eyes met, and Peter went out and wept bitterly.

We usually assume that the cockcrow was the sound of a rooster. But that may not be the case at all. The house of the High Priest was located in the heart of Jerusalem and, according to Jewish law, poultry would not be allowed in the holy city. They might defile the holy place. The changing of the Roman guard took place at 3:00 a.m. At the change of the guard, a trumpet sounded to signal that change. This trumpet call was literally called a "cock-crow."[1] At the moment of the sounding of the trumpet and of the changing of the sentry, Peter remembered that our Lord had told him that he would deny him three times. And he had.

This story is surprising! It is amazing that it is in the New Testament. After all, Peter was a hero and leader in the early church.

---

1   William Barclay, *The Gospel of Matthew*, vol. 2 (Philadelphia: The Westminster Press, 1958), 382-383.

Other than Jesus, Simon Peter's name occurs more often in the gospels than anyone else. This story records Peter's absolute failure in the face of his first real test in following his Lord. Peter also on other occasions had **mis**understood the real meaning of Jesus' teaching, which on one time, Jesus told him to "get you behind me, Satan" as Peter misinterpreted what Jesus had said. Look at what his story tells us about Peter and ourselves.

SIMON PETER'S WEAKNESS

This story begins by acknowledging Peter's weakness. This story could be in the New Testament for only one reason. Peter had told it to others. There was no other disciple present that night. Peter was the only disciple that went into the courtyard to see what would happen to Jesus. All the rest of them had fled. Peter had courage enough to risk his own life as he followed his Lord. This story is autobiographical. Peter boldly shared his failure in the moment of his temptation. But what a testimony it must have been to the early church to know that the one who had been described as a rock had slipped and fallen. If Christ had forgiven him, how much more could there be an opportunity for others to know forgiveness and experience a new beginning.

There were likely several reasons Peter denied Jesus that night. If he was not afraid for his life, he did not want to be ridiculed. Many of us do not want to face ridicule as a Christian. He also was filled with questions and doubts now about Jesus and whether he was really the long-looked-for Messiah. But he was likely afraid for his life. If Jesus was being charged with sedition against the Roman government, then his disciples might also be arrested and charged with a similar crime.

OVERCONFIDENCE

One of the main reasons Peter failed, however, I believe, was because he was overconfident. He had thought that he could withstand whatever came his way. When Jesus predicted the suffering and difficulties which lay before him, Peter stood up and with a ringing cry said: "Lord, if everybody else forsakes you, I never will." He did not recognize his weakness. We cannot act as though we have no weaknesses. There are temptations that we cannot master with our own resources.

We often think that we are tempted at our weakest point, and sometimes we are. But some of our most devastating temptations confront us at what we think is our greatest strength. Here is a husky male who always brags about his strength and courage. When a fire sweeps through their house, who is it that rushes in and rescues the child? Why, it's the small, weak, timid mother. The husband stands back petrified, unable to move in the face of danger, while she steps forward. A person may appear to be strong, but he/she may not be able to use that strength when it is needed. Our overconfidence may cause us to stumble and fall. Peter did the thing he hated and what he thought he would not do. He meant to do good but did wrong.

When he realized his failure, he fled and wept bitterly. But he did not give way to despair as Judas did and go out and hang himself. His weeping led to repentance and a changed life. The tears of Peter were the tears of someone who realized that he had done the very thing he thought he would never do. He was not only unfaithful to his Lord, but he had been unfaithful to the highest in himself. He wept bitter tears because of his failure. But you and I have shed tears because of lost hopes and dreams, misplaced priorities, lost opportunity, unkind words, angry reactions, being too busy to listen, too self-satisfied to learn, unwilling to take the time we needed, or we simply did not feel deeply enough for someone else's pain, hurt or grief. We, too, must shed tears for our failures, sins, and abuses. Like Peter, we too should weep.

WE MAY ALSO DENY JESUS

Peter had denied his Lord, but so have you, and so have I. Who among us, at some time or another, through a word, some inappropriate action, something not done or said, has denied our

Lord in the office, in the factory, at school, at home, at play, or at some time or other. At some place, at some moment, we have denied our Lord and refused to be recognized as his disciple. We were ashamed of the best that we have ever experienced, and we gave in to the lowest dominion in our lives. It is easy to do, isn't it? But the realization that this is possible for us is the first step toward combating the temptations that can drag us down and destroy us.

One Sunday morning as an Episcopal church gathered for worship, a bum stumbled in and sat down on the back pew. The congregation was reciting the general confession. He heard them say: "We have left undone those things which we ought to have done, and we have done those things which we ought not to have done, and there is no health in us." The bum dropped down in the nearest pew and exclaimed, "Obviously, this is my crowd!"

We, like this bum, recognize the truth about our own failures. There are those things which have been left undone, which we needed to do, and there are those things which we have done, which we have to confess we should not have done. We know we are guilty, and we are ashamed. We have discovered that the power to forgive is not in ourselves. It must come from the Lord. Peter acknowledged his own failure in the courtyard and the forgiving grace of Christ which he later experienced. He repeated this story and told others so they might know about this same kind of forgiveness.

Years ago, in Aberdeen, Scotland, a noted preacher named Brownlow North was preaching in one of the churches in the city, and right before he was to go into the pulpit, he was handed a letter. The letter was from a man in the city, who recounted a shameful incident in North's past, and told him if he dared to go into the pulpit that day, he was going to rise in the congregation and tell everybody what North had done. Brownlow North had lived a wild life as a young man before he became a Christian. North walked into the pulpit and read the letter to the congregation. He told them that what this man said was true. But he told them about the good news of Jesus Christ that changed his life. He spoke of Christ's forgiveness and how his past was put behind him and he was able to begin a new life. He used his own failure to point other persons to Christ.

The good news for each of us who has sinned is that we can find forgiveness and the possibility of beginning anew in Jesus Christ. Peter was willing to acknowledge his weakness. By acknowledging his failure, he experienced forgiveness.

PETER ACCEPTED THE CHALLENGE

Go another step further and you notice that Peter accepted the challenge which Jesus gave him. In the twenty-first chapter of the Gospel of John, the writer has recorded the experience where Peter and six other disciples met the resurrected Christ on the shore of the Sea of Tiberias. This is the place where Jesus turned to Simon Peter and asked him three times: "Simon, do you love me?" Three times Peter had denied his Lord, and now three times Jesus asked him, "Peter, do you love me?" The word that Jesus uses for love in Greek asked for a higher spiritual commitment than the responding word for love with which Peter replied. The questions to Peter seemed to be on a diminishing scale: "Do you love me more than these?" "Do you love me?" "Are you my friend?"

On the third time, Jesus used Peter's own word for love and asked him if he loved him even on the level of a friend. "Simon, son of John, are you even my friend at all?" Although painfully aware of his weakness, and deeply grieved at the repetition of the question, Peter avowed that, even though he did once deny his Lord, he affirmed the reality of his love for Jesus. Crying out he declared: "Lord, you know all things, and you know that I love you." Each time Jesus told Peter, "Feed my sheep," "Pastor my people."

Rather than acknowledge our failures, sins, or denials, many of us offer excuses. We are like Pierre in Tolstoy's novel, *War and Peace,* who was pressed to face his own mistakes. His response sounds like many of us, "Yes, Lord, I have sinned, but I have several excellent excuses." We all have many excuses for our actions, don't we?

Like Flip Wilson, we often want to say, "The devil made me do it." Several years ago, there was a cartoon showing a woman who had bought an expensive dress. When her husband asked why she had been so extravagant, she replied: "The devil made me do it." "Well," the husband asked, "Why didn't you say, 'Get thee behind me, Satan'"? "I did," the wife responded. "But he said the dress looked as good in the back as in the front, so I bought it."

Excuses ... We are often like the little boy in the schoolyard when a teacher broke up a fight between him and another boy and asked, "Who started it?" "He started it when he hit me back," he exclaimed. Excuses of all kinds!

Rather than excuses, like Peter, we must acknowledge our failures, sins, and denials before we can experience forgiveness. That is the important first step. We are always in process of being made whole. None of us has arrived in his or her spiritual growth. Confess your weaknesses so you can grow deeper in the faith.

Jesus forgave Peter for his denial and then gave him a challenge and responsibility to go and minister in his name. He had denied his Lord but that was not the end of life. Jesus forgave him and he entrusted him to serve in his name. Later Peter became one of the great heroes and ministers in the early Christian church. Here was a man whose confidence and self-worth had been devastated in that encounter in the High Priest's courtyard. Peter felt that he had turned his back on his Lord, and he had hated the action that he had taken. Like many of us who have sinned, he wished he could undo what he had done, but it was too late. It was over and done.

In Jesus Christ, we find the restoration of real personhood. From our sin, we are forgiven and cleansed. We can take pride in who we are because we have the assurance of God's creative and redeeming love. No matter what we may have been or done, Christ can change our lives and give us a new beginning through his love. Like Peter, we, too, can know forgiveness and the summons to serve our Lord again. Faith commitment is challenging and demanding and never without its questions. Nevertheless, like Jon Meacham, we acknowledge that "For me, faith is complicated, challenging, and sometimes confounding. It is not magical but mysterious."[2] We bow our knees before the mystery of God's presence and seek to follow our Lord's "call" in quiet trust.

PETER'S VISION WAS RESTORED

Peter also found that his vision was restored. When he started following Jesus Christ, he was among the first of the disciples to commit his life to the Lord. He believed that Jesus Christ was going to usher in the kingdom of God. He had become a "fisher of men" to help Jesus Christ initiate God's reign. When Jesus was nailed to the cross, Peter thought that his dream was over and done with. But the resurrected Christ restored his dream. Christ forgave Peter for denying him and gave him a new commission. He restored Peter's vision about the kingdom of God. Sometimes I see people in church some of whom gave their lives to Christ a long time ago. But their vision has become dull and faded. Their involvement in the work of Christ and his church has become lean. These persons need to recapture their dreams and have their vision restored so they can see once again the possibilities for our world as they serve in Christ's kingdom.

Give yourself to some cause that will outlast you. Give yourself to something more meaningful than just things. Invest your life in the service of Christ and one day you will discover that you have committed your life to something that will still be going on when you die. Peter accepted the challenge of Christ and gave himself to serve in his kingdom. His vision and dream continue today through your service and mine.

PETER AFFIRMED HIS FAITH

Notice finally that Peter affirmed his faith by his life. He had denied Christ in the courtyard of the High Priest. When confronted by the maidservant and others, he denied his Christ. Can you

---

2   Jon Meacham, *The Hope of Glory: Reflections on the Last Words of Jesus from the Cross* (New York: Convergent Books, 2020), 96.

not imagine the fear that leaped in Peter's heart the first time the question was asked him: "Are you one of his followers?" He probably wanted to slip into a dark corner or run away. Would you have stayed? Before you condemn Peter for denying Christ, ask yourself whether you would have stayed nearby after Jesus was arrested. You would have to fear not only the crucifixion of Jesus but likely your own death. When he was asked, "Are you not one of his disciples?" he denied it. But he did not run. He stayed nearby in the courtyard. But he had denied Christ with his words and action.

The crowing of the rooster or the sounding of the "cock-crow" was an announcement that dawn was approaching. As the light of dawn broke, Peter realized that his rash promises had been broken and his cocky spirit was unrealistic. Through his tears began the dawning of a new day for him. This dawning would not be fully realized until he saw the risen Christ, but this "cock-crow" was a new beginning for him.

Later after Peter was forgiven and commissioned into discipleship, he served his Lord through his words, teachings, and even his death. Tradition states that Peter was crucified later in Rome. And he was crucified upside down because he did not want to be crucified just like his Lord. Through his words and life, he later demonstrated his faith.

Jesus said, "You will know my disciples by their fruits." "You are living epistles," the New Testament writer wrote of the early Christians, "And you are known and read by others." The way you live demonstrates what kind of Christian faith you have. Later, Peter put his life where his words had been.

In his book, *Dr. Schweitzer of Lambarene,* Norman Cousins tells about the regular practice the jungle hospital had following the evening meal. The famous doctor would sit down and play some hymns on an upright piano on the other side of the room where they ate. The piano, Cousins notes, had to be at least fifty years old. The keyboard was badly stained and most of the ivory was fastened by double screws to each key. The strings were missing on at least a dozen keys. Under the extreme heat and moisture of Africa, it was impossible to keep the piano in tune.

Now one of the greatest musicians in the world and the greatest living interpreter of Bach's organ music, sat down to play on this old dilapidated instrument. But Cousins notes that "the amazing and wondrous thing was that the piano seemed to lose its poverty in his hands. Whatever its capacity was to yield music was now being fully realized. The tininess and chattering echoes seemed subdued. It may be that this was the result of Schweitzer's intimate acquaintance with the piano, enabling him to avoid the rebellious keys and favoring only the cooperative ones. Whatever the reason, his being at the piano strangely seemed to make it right."[3]

This is for me a parable about our life when it comes under the Master's touch. No matter why we have sinned or denied our Lord, whether through ignorance, apathy, weakness, pride, arrogance, overconfidence, or yielding to temptation, when we come under our Master's touch, our lives are made new again. Jesus forgives our sins and failures and offers us new life. It is the dawn of a new day for us, as it was for Simon Peter. May God give us the strength to respond.

O God, we acknowledge that we have failed or denied you in so many ways. Give us the courage to accept your grace and to respond to your forgiving love. In the name of Christ, we pray. Amen.

---

3   Norman Cousins, *Dr. Schweitzer of Lambarene* (New York: Harper & Brothers, 1960), 10.

4.

THE POURING OF WATER:

PILATE'S INDECISION

Matthew 27:24-26

There is a fascinating painting by Michael Munkacsy entitled "Christ before Pilate" which was finished in 1881. The painting gives the appearance of a Grand Opera with all of the main players and chorus assembled for the final scene. This scene is set in the Praetorium Judgment Hall of Pilate. On the right side of the painting is a figure of Pilate, the Procurator, sitting on a throne. Below him are benches where Roman judges usually sit, but in the picture, they are filled with Pharisees, who are members of the Jewish religious body. These "doctors of the law" are whispering to each other and seem to be looking with contempt upon the prisoner Jesus. To the left of Jesus, a Roman soldier, dressed in his military attire, including a helmet, holds back the crowd with a spear. The faces of the angry crowd telegraph a message of condemnation through their frowns and scoffing demeanor. One of the persons in the crowd leans mockingly into the face of Jesus, while another seems to be jumping up and down yelling frantically, "Crucify him. Crucify him!" The only supportive face in the crowd is that of a young mother with a child in her arms, a sort of "Madonna" figure.

The crowd presses forward as Caiaphas, the Jewish High Priest, stands before Pilate making a condemning speech about the "insurrection" of Jesus. Pilate is seated on his judgment seat clothed in a white toga with a purple border indicating the dress of a Roman senator. Behind him on the throne are the wreath and insignia, symbols of the power of Rome. Pilate appears to be only half-listening to Caiaphas' speech and his eyes are fixed on his hands as he seems to be rubbing them together.

Jesus stands in the middle of this painting looking haggard from the strain of this emotional and physical ordeal. Nevertheless, he stands straight in a white robe. His appearance communicates strength and calmness in the midst of chaos and confusion. Although he is the one on trial, his probing stare at Pilate calls into question who is really on trial here.

For centuries Christians have proclaimed in the Apostles Creed that Jesus "suffered under Pontius Pilate." That notation has assured an obscure governor in a remote part of the world a continuing place in history. Pilate's name has been forever linked with Jesus. Several years ago, a French writer and lawyer, named Jacques Isori, wrote a book, *The True Trial of Jesus*. In his book, he tried to absolve the Jewish leaders from the crucifixion of Jesus and put the blame on the Roman government who found Jesus guilty of insurrection and put him to death by crucifixion according to Roman law. Pilate was a chief participant in this drama.

Pilate was likely appointed procurator of Judea in A.D. 26, about three years before Jesus was crucified. He probably received this appointment because he was married to Claudia Procula, who was the illegitimate daughter of the third wife of Tiberius Caesar. Pilate was noted for his arrogance, bad temper, cruelty, and insulting behavior. He despised the Jews and they had no reason to consider him a great leader.

SEVERAL ROMAN OFFENCES TO THE JEWS

Three incidents indicate the reason relationships between the Jews and Pilate were so strained. When he marched the Roman troops into Jerusalem, unlike other rulers who tried to honor the *Jewish aversion to graven images*, he allowed the soldiers to bring their standards into the city with their metal images of the emperor on them. The Jews were so outraged that they surrounded the palace in Caesarea, several thousand strong, and prayed loudly to God for six days that the images be removed. After six days, Pilate told the Jews to meet him in the marketplace where he would speak to them. When they got there, he surrounded the marketplace with soldiers and told them that unless they stopped protesting, he would massacre all of them. Many of the soldiers were Samaritans and would have enjoyed killing the Jews. But the Jewish leaders laid on the ground and laid bare their necks and proclaimed: "It is better to die than to have images in Jerusalem." Pilate recanted because he knew that a massacre of thousands of unarmed Jews would not please Tiberius, and soon he would lose his position as governor.

Another time he *hung a series of shields in the palace in Jerusalem bearing the images of Roman gods*. The Jewish priests took their protests to Emperor Tiberius, and he ordered Pilate to remove them. A third episode occurred when Pilate *used money from the Temple treasury to pay for a new water system* for Jerusalem. The Jews led a rebellion because of this action and many of them were killed. Pilate received a harsh rebuke from Rome for his action. The Jewish people hated Pilate and Pilate despised them.

WHAT SHALL WE DO WITH JESUS?

Before this Roman official, Jesus was put on trial. The final question of the Gospel of Matthew is raised in Pilate's words: "What shall I do with Jesus called the Christ?" That question continues to demand our attention. Look at several ways Pilate responded to his own question.

Avoid a Decision

First, Pilate tried to avoid making a decision. He tried hard not to get involved with the Jews and their conflict with Jesus. Pilate detested the Jewish leaders who were subject to Rome and yet thought themselves too pure to enter a Roman house. They did not want to be defiled by entering the house of a Gentile. When Pilate was awakened by the clamor of the Jewish leaders, he asked them, "What accusation do you bring against this man?" "If he were not a criminal," they replied, "We should not have brought him before you." Pilate, sensing this was a matter of their own petty laws, and thinking he could avoid a decision, declared; "Take him away and try him by your own law" (John 18:31). But the priests indicated their intentions when they said, "We are not allowed to put any man to death."

When Pilate questioned Jesus and declared that he found no fault in him, the Jewish leaders stated that he had stirred up all the people in Judea from Galilee to Jerusalem. Hearing that Jesus was from Galilee, Pilate knew that Galilee was not under his jurisdiction but under Herod, who was presently in Jerusalem. So quickly he sent Jesus in chains to Herod, thinking that he had avoided another problem with these pesky Jews. But in a short period of time, he heard the roar of the crowd again as Jesus was once again brought back to his palace.

Let the Crowd Decide

This time Pilate thought of another way to avoid facing his own question about Christ. He would let the crowd decide. It had been the Roman custom to release a prisoner at Passover time as a gesture to the Jews. One of his prisoners was named Jesus Barabbas, a political revolutionary. He was a murderer and a known insurrectionist. He would let the people choose between Jesus of Nazareth and Jesus Barabbas. So, he asked them: "Which of the two do you wish me to release to you?" "Barabbas," they cried." "Then what am I to do with Jesus called Christ?" he asked them. "Crucify him!" they screamed.

WE HAVE TO DECIDE

Pilate had tried evasion, but it had not worked. And that is true for us as well. We have to decide. Deciding not to decide is to decide. We cannot remain neutral. We must make a choice. Life is filled with choices. Not to make a choice is to choose.

If I am coming down the Ohio River in a boat and I am trying to decide whether I will get off at Louisville or not, I must make a decision. Even if I continue debating the issue, a decision will be made. The current of the river will take me past Louisville if I do not choose to embark. The river current will be operative whether I choose or not. I can choose to dock my boat, or the current will take me south.

We are confronted by the presence of Jesus. What will we do with Jesus called the Christ? Will we simply admire him as a great teacher, healer, friend, or a good man and not make a commitment? Many today try to avoid making a decision about Christ by ignoring him. They will not be unkind or harmful, but they want to remain indifferent. Studdert-Kennedy, the English clergyman, has expressed that truth in these lines:

When Jesus came to Birmingham, they simply passed Him by,
They never hurt a hair of Him, they only let Him die;
For men had grown more tender, and they would not give Him pain,
They only just passed down the street and left Him in the rain.[1]
We, like Pilate, want to avoid making a decision.

---

1   Leonard Cutts, editor, *The Best of G. A. Studdert-Kennedy* (London: Hodder & Stoughton Limited, 1951), 210.

A Compromise

But Pilate was faced again with the question: "What shall I do with Jesus called the Christ?" Go a step further with me and notice that Pilate attempted a course of compromise. He had asked Jesus: "Are you the king of the Jews?" "Is that your own idea or has someone suggested it to you?" Jesus replied. According to John's Gospel, Jesus stated further that his kingdom was not of this world (John 18:36).

Upon questioning him Pilate declared, "I find no case against him." But, after declaring that Jesus was innocent, Pilate does a strange thing. Rather than setting Jesus free, Pilate offers the religious leaders a compromise. He thought that if he had Jesus scourged it might appease their anger. Scourging itself was an awful torture. A prisoner was beaten forty times with a heavy leather whip, which often contained bits of metal or bone to cut more deeply into the back of the one being lashed. Many persons died from the lashing alone.

After the severe beating, some of the soldiers plaited a crown of thorns and pressed it painfully upon his brow and blood dripped down upon his forehead. Then they put a purple robe upon him and knelt in mockery before him and cried: "Hail, King of the Jews!" Thinking that this compromise had satisfied the religious leaders, Pilate brought Jesus before them and said, "Behold the man." He seemed to be saying to them, "See by his weakened appearance that this Jesus is no longer a threat to you. I find no case against him. This is enough. Go home!" But the suffering of Jesus under the stinging lash was not enough. The chief priests and the crowd yelled, "Crucify him! Crucify Him!"

WHY DID PILATE RESPOND AS HE DID?

Pilate's behavior in this episode seems unlike previous images of him. Why was this man, who had on other occasions been so merciless, now so cautious? There could be at least *three reasons.* One was *the dream of his wife*, Claudia. She had sent a letter to

Pilate by her slave which read: "Have nothing to do with that innocent man; I was much troubled on his account in my dreams last night." Romans took dreams very seriously and Pilate likely was troubled by this warning.

Second, *Jesus' demeanor was probably disturbing to Pilate.* Throughout all the accusations and hostility, Jesus remained calm and serene. His answer to Pilate's question had been brief and during most of the questions, Jesus remained silent. Pilate had likely not witnessed such composure during this kind of ordeal before.

Third, Pilate was afraid that if this *disturbance got out of hand,* Tiberius would hear about it and his position as governor might be in question. He wanted the friendship and goodwill of Tiberius and the last thing he wanted was a riot from the Jews during Passover. That could end his career. He figured that it was better for one man's life to be sacrificed than to have a rebellion on his hands. No one Jewish man was worth that to him, innocent or not. He wanted to stay in good favor with these Jewish leaders so they would not create a problem for him with the emperor. He felt he had tried hard to release Jesus but even his compromise scourging had not been enough.

Transferring Responsibility

Go with me one final step in our drama and notice that Pilate tried to answer the question, "What shall I do with Jesus called the Christ?" by transferring responsibility. He decided not to accept responsibility for the decision but to "pass the buck" to others. He asked for a basin of water to be brought in and he washed his hands before the religious leaders and the crowd. "My hands are clean of this man's blood," he declared. "See to that yourselves." With a united cry, they accepted the responsibility as they spoke with one voice: "His blood be on us, and on our children."

But can responsibility be so easily passed on to another? Pilate could not transfer his guilt to another scapegoat. He had the responsibility as a governor to act wisely according to Roman law.

He chose not to. He was not free from guilt by washing his hands. This buck could not be handed to another without sharing in the blame. But neither could the Jewish leaders or the crowd. They chose to crucify an innocent man, rather than have their religious viewpoint challenged. The stain of innocent blood was indeed on their hands as well as Pilate's.

Many have tried to say with Pilate, "I've washed my hands of it," whatever "it" might be. "I am innocent of this matter. Someone else is to blame." Persons at the Nuremberg trials, the hearings for the Vietnam War, the Watergate conspiracy, the Iran-contra cover-up, the S and L scandal, corporate business failures, etc., have blamed others and transferred the accountability to someone else. Rather than seeing the stain on our own hands, we choose to blame our parents, children, schools, politicians, blacks, whites, or unions, corporations, the press, the media, heredity, the environment, crooks, drug dealers, the young or old, lack of education, not enough experience, too little time, our age or youth and on and on the list goes. Our minds and mouths are filled with excuses, pretenses, and blame. But this does not wash our responsibility away. But as Lady Macbeth came to realize the "spot" of guilt cannot so easily be washed away. Pilate's gesture of washing his hands of this matter was futile.

In Switzerland, the grandeur of Mount Pilatus, named after Pilate, raises its lofty peaks above lovely Lake Lucerne. According to legend, Pilate's body was buried somewhere on that mountain, and on every moonlit night, the restless spirit of Pilate hovers over the waters of the lake forever washing his hands. His shame and guilt continue.

Walter Rauschenbusch has written that on the eve of the crucifixion of Jesus, the wash-basin of Pilate disappeared from the palace. No one knows who took it. But since that moment the washbowl has been abroad in the land as men and women continually wash their hands to absolve themselves of responsibility. The pouring of water is heard everywhere. Its sound is repeated in the refusal to accept responsibility for peace in Northern Ireland, in the ongoing conflict between Israel and Palestine, in the prejudice between whites and blacks, the man who abuses small children, the parents who turn their heads while their son shoplifts and cheats in school, or the "Christian" employer who steals from her company, a husband who is unfaithful to his marriage vow, the rich exploiting the poor, or the politician who accepts favors. All of these and others are busy using Pilate's washbowl. Listen to the sound of the water as it pours. Can you hear it?

PILATE'S WASH BOWL AND JESUS' BOWL

In contrast to Pilate's bowl of evasion of responsibility, notice the towel and basin Jesus used in the Upper Room. Pilate's bowl symbolizes a desire to escape problems and burdens. Jesus' basin represents service. In life, we are faced with these choices. Which basin will you choose — the one to avoid struggles or the one which denotes ministry? The towel and basin of our Lord challenge us to be concerned about the needs of others and realize our tie with all of humanity.

OUR QUESTION TODAY

The question, "What shall I do with Jesus called the Christ?" still echoes down through the centuries. It is your question and mine today. The New Testament rings with the words that men and women said about him and claims Jesus made for himself. He is the Son of David, Son of God, Son of man, Messiah, the Servant of God, the Good Shepherd, the Divine Physician, the Savior, the Prophet, King, the Stone, Bridegroom, the Bread of Life, the Light of the World, the Door, the Vine, the Way, the Truth, the Life, the Resurrection and the Life, the Judge, the Lamb, the Scapegoat, the High Priest, the Just one, the Amen, the Alpha and Omega, the Beginning and End, the Head, the Image, the Christ of Creation, the Firstborn of Creation, the Bright and Morning Star, and others.

Who is he? He is Lord of your life if you will open it to him. "What shall I do with Jesus called the Christ?" The question demanded an answer. The disciples could not remain neutral. They had to decide. They had to choose. Whenever Jesus Christ comes into your life or my life, we can no longer remain neutral. We must either accept or reject him. He expects a decision and response. That does not mean we have all the answers about religion or that our faith is not sometimes shaky. We seek to respond with the best we have at the given moment. "A commitment of faith is a commitment to stick with it through all the various seasons of faith and even those moments when faith is absent," writes David Brooks. "To commit to faith is to commit to the long series of ups and downs, to institutions, learning and forgetting, knowing one sort of God when you're thirty-five, fifty-five, and seventy-five."[2] We make a commitment and continue to trust throughout our journey through life. We cannot ignore Christ. "What shall I do with Jesus called the Christ?" is now a question directed to you and me. Martin Luther once wrote: "I care not whether he be Christ, but that he be Christ for you!" Admiration is not enough. There must be adoration. When Christ confronts us, if we know who he is, we will fall at his feet and say with Thomas: "My Lord and my God."

We are still confronted with the question today: "What shall I do with Jesus called the Christ?" Like Pilate, we can try to avoid making a decision, or seek a compromise, or try to pass the buck to another. Some try to settle for admiration; while others ignore or reject him. But, as we learn from Pilate, we cannot avoid making a decision. Not deciding is to decide. We must make a choice.

ANOTHER LOOK AT MUNKACSY'S PAINTING

Return with me now to the painting by Munkacsy where we began. Several years ago, in Hamilton, Ontario there was an exhibit of Munkacsy's "Christ before Pilate." A sailor from the lake boats approached the door of the exhibit hall and asked: "Is Christ here? How much to see Christ?"

---

2   David Brooks, *The Second Mountain: The Quest for a Moral Life* (New York: Random House, 2019), 249.

When he was told the admission fee, he complained, "Well, I suppose I'll have to pay it." He put down his money and swaggered into the room. He sat down in front of the great picture and studied it a moment or two, and presently he took off his hat. He gazed upon it a little longer, and then, leaning down, he picked up the description catalog which he had dropped when he took his seat. He read it over and studied the painting anew, dropping his face into his hands at intervals. He remained for a full hour. When he came out there were tears in his eyes, and suppressed sobs in his voice as he said:

> "Madam, I came here to see Christ because my mother asked me to. I am a rough man sailing on the Lakes, and before I went on this cruise my mother wanted me to see this picture, and I came to please her. I never believed in any such thing, but the man who could paint a picture like that— he must have believed in it. And there is something in it that makes me believe in it too."[3]

We, too, are confronted by Christ, and he calls us to make a commitment. Will you wash your hands of him or choose to follow him as Lord? The decision is yours and mine.

O God, we struggle to wash our hands of so many things in life. Give us the courage to accept our responsibility for service and commitment. Through Christ, who gave his all for us, we pray. Amen.

---

3   Cynthia Peral Maus, *Christ and the Fine Arts* (New York: Harper & Brothers, 1938), 363.

5.

THE POUNDING OF THE HAMMER:

JESUS' DEATH

Matthew 27:33-37

Recently I read a strange story about a man named Menelik, II, who was the Emperor of Ethiopia from 1889 to 1913. He heard about a new method the West had of executing hardened criminals with a device called the electric chair. He thought that this would be a useful thing for his country. So, he ordered an electric chair, and one was sent to Ethiopia. There was only one problem — there was no electricity in Ethiopia at that time. Nobody had bothered to tell him that he needed electricity to make an electric chair work! He decided that he would not waste his new purchase. He modified the electric chair slightly and turned it into a throne.[1]

---

1   Clifton Fadiman, editor. *The Little, Brown Book of Anecdotes* (Boston: Little, Brown and Co., 1985), 396.

That seems like a strange story indeed. Yet, the Christian church has done almost the same thing to that method of ancient execution, which was a cross. That ancient method of execution, the slow torturous death on a cross, has been turned into a throne. Christians have pointed to the cross down through the centuries as the place where God has reigned supremely.

THE CENTRAL SYMBOL OF THE CHRISTIAN RELIGION

The cross is the central symbol of our faith. This symbol of the cross is seen on top of church buildings, on church altars, or in stained glass windows, and other places. Crosses are often imprinted on Bibles and hymn books. The Christian flag and the flags of some nations bear the symbol of the cross. Some churches are designed in the shape of a cross. The cross is also worn sometimes as a lapel pin or on a necklace. I have also seen crosses made of chocolate, roses, and other flowers.

When you turn to the New Testament, you will find that there is an awful, stark reality about the dreadfulness of the cross. Jesus came into Jerusalem on what you and I call Palm Sunday to the shouts of hosanna from the people. It seemed to be a wonderful, joyous time. Then Jesus cleansed the Temple, and later celebrated the Passover or what the church came to call the Lord's Supper in the Upper Room with his disciples. He knelt in Gethsemane and prayed that "the cup" which lay before him might be removed. He was betrayed, arrested, went through a mock trial, was flogged, and then finally was crucified in a place called Golgotha.

I have found any attempt to write or preach about the cross of Jesus Christ and the meaning of our Lord's death is not easy. I always struggle to put into words the meaning of this death, because for me it has always been shrouded in mystery and awe. I have had no easy words to explain it. I always approach this event with feet of humility. John Milton wrote a beautiful poem entitled, "On the Morning of Christ's Nativity," in celebration of the birth of Jesus. When he tried to write poetry about the death of Christ, he could not put his feelings into words because the mystery so overwhelmed him.

One of the great theologians of the past century, Paul Tillich, approached the death of Christ by drawing upon the artistic symbolisms which were expressed by the New Testament writers. With a skilled brush, the biblical artists painted symbols about the sun which veiled its face in shame at the horror which caused this death. The curtain of the Temple was rent as a symbol that everyone now could come directly to God. The earth seemed to be shaken as it was judged by the death on the cross this day. The dead were raised. Nature seemed to have received a new meaning. History was transformed, and no one was any longer what he or she was before because of this event.[2]

THE CROSS AT THE CENTER OF PAUL'S PREACHING

The Apostle Paul did not hesitate to put the cross of Jesus Christ right at the center of his preaching. He wrote to the Corinthians, "For I decided to know nothing among you except Jesus Christ and him crucified (2 Corinthians 2:2). Writing to the Galatians, "God forbid that I should glory, save in the cross of our Lord Jesus Christ" (Galatians 6:14). Writing to the Philippian church, Paul declared, "Though Jesus was in the form of God, he did not count equality with God a thing to be grasped, but emptied himself, taking the form of a servant and became obedient unto death, even the death on a cross" (Philippians 2:6-8).

Where did Paul get this focus on the cross? It has been at the center of the teaching of the early church. One-fourth of the material in the Gospels focuses on the death of Jesus Christ. Matthew and Mark dedicate one-third of their gospels to the death of Jesus. In Luke, it is one-fourth. In John, half of that gospel focuses on the last twenty-four hours of the life of Jesus. In most biographies, the writers give only a few paragraphs or maybe a few pages, and

---

2   Paul Tillich, *The New Being* (New York: Charles Scribner's Sons, 1955), 175-176.

sometimes only a line or two is devoted to the death of the One about whom the book is written. But the gospel writers realized that the death of Jesus was so startling, offensive, and pivotal to the Jewish expectation of the Messiah that they had to address it.

In Dorothy Sayers' play, "The Man Born to Be King," Jesus is brought to the place where he is to be crucified. Before he is nailed to the cross, one of the soldiers offers Jesus a drug to deaden the pain.

> "Here, my lad — don't be obstinate. Drink it. It'll dead-en you like. You won't feel so much. No? Come on, then, get down to it."

The first soldier is less humane:
"Stretch your legs. I'll give you king of the Jews."
"Hand me the mallet."
"Father, forgive them. They don't know what they are doing."

Then the voice of Jesus fades off as the pounding of the hammer begins as the soldiers drive the seven-inch nails into the lower part of the forearm between the ulnar and radial bones. Several years ago, some archaeologists discovered the bones of a crucified man and found that the nails were not driven into the palms of the hands but the forearm. His feet were placed together, and a nail was driven through the heel bones. In this horrid way, Jesus was fastened to the cross.

THE PHYSICAL DEATH OF JESUS

Should we focus primarily upon the physical death of Jesus? A few years ago, a medical doctor in our church sent me a copy of an article in the *Journal of the American Medical Association* which described the physical agony of Jesus when he was crucified.[3] I would not minimize the physical death of Jesus for a moment. It is interesting to me, however, that when the New Testament writes

---

3   *The Journal of the American Medical Association* (March 21, 1986. Vol. 255, No. 11), 1455-1463.

about Jesus' crucifixion, two words, one word in Greek, describe his death. Only two words! They are translated in English as "Having been crucified." The gospel writers did not focus that much upon the physical act of his death. According to historians, thousands of other persons have been crucified this way. Josephus, the Jewish historian, recorded that two thousand persons were crucified during a rebellion in Galilee against the Roman government. On another day, eight hundred Jews were crucified during a civil war. Sometimes so many persons were crucified by the Roman armies that the crosses of those crucified overlapped each other on the road.

Are we saved by crosses? Are we saved by crucifixions? Is it just the physical death of Jesus that redeems us? No. Salvation has to come from One whose cross pointed beyond the death of the one hanging there. There was something unique about this One who was crucified. The New Testament rings with the affirmation that the One on this particular cross was the Incarnate One. God was in Christ. This cross could not contain the One who was crucified. Death was not the end for him.

JESUS' DEATH IS A PARADOX

The death of Christ has always been a great paradox. In one sense, the life of Jesus was a life taken by the Romans as they crucified him, but it was also a life given. Jesus was a victim but also a victor. Here we see horror and glory, wickedness, and sacrifice. The cross showed humanity at its worst and humanity at its best. The cross represents, for us, sacrifice and the One who is the high priest. It represents despair and hope, murder, betrayal, and rejection, but it also depicts love, sacrifice, and grace.

Jesus Christ spoke boldly that his life was not simply being taken, but that he was giving it willingly. "For this reason, the Father loves me," Jesus said, "because I lay down my life that I may take it again. No one takes it from me, but I lay it down of my own accord and I have the power to lay it down and I have power to take it up again; this charge I have from my Father" (John 10:17-18). In Mark's gospel, we read: "The Son of Man came also not

to be served, but to serve, and to give his life a ransom for many"
(Mark 10:45). Jesus had predicted his death. But the disciples had
not been able to hear it. They had either not wanted to or could
not hear it. After all, they had looked for something other than a
Suffering Messiah. Who wanted a Suffering Messiah? They wanted a political king, somebody who would overthrow the Roman
government and give them freedom from tyranny.

THE SUFFERING SERVANT

Many in Judaism saw Isaiah's picture as one of Israel itself. Jesus might be seen as a type of Israel himself. But they may not have
read Isaiah very carefully, had they? In Isaiah's picture of the Suffering Servant, the verbs alone give us an image of the Suffering One
who will come as Messiah. Notice the verbs: He will be marred,
recoiled, shut-mouthed, rootless, formless, charmless, despised,
rejected, pained, avoided, afflicted, bore our sufferings, endured
our torments, smitten by God, struck down by disease and misery,
wounded, bruised, chastised, crushed, oppressed, dumb, stricken to
death, numbered with transgressors, bore the sins of many, offered
for sin, poured out his soul, and made his grave with the wicked.
These words vibrate with the heartbeat of a suffering God.

Listen to Paul as he writes in I Corinthians the first chapter:
"The doctrine of the cross is sheer folly to those on their way to
ruin... Jews call for miracles, Greeks look for wisdom, but we
proclaim Christ: Yes, Christ nailed to the cross; and though this
is a stumbling block to Jews and folly to Greeks, yet to those who
have heard his call, Jews and Greeks alike, he is the power of God
and the wisdom of God" (1 Corinthians 1:18, 22-24).

CRUCIFIXION: A STUMBLING BLOCK

Paul did not hesitate to say that this Messiah was not a political
figure. He knew that to the Jews crucifixion was a stumbling block
because of their belief that it was cursed to be crucified (Deuter-
onomy 21:23). This talk about a crucified Messiah was a barrier

many Jews could not get beyond. To the Greek mind, the concept of a crucified, incarnate God was sheer foolishness. They could not imagine a crucified God.

To the Greek mind, God could not suffer. Lucian's *Dialogues of the Dead* illustrates this view clearly. King Philip of Macedon chastises his son Alexander for rejecting his human father and claiming to be a god. "Have you nothing to say of my adventuresome spirit when I led an attack and was covered with wounds?" Alexander replies. "That would be all very well for a king's son," Philip observes, "but this was the last thing you were called upon to do. You were passing for a god, and your being wounded and carried off the field in a litter, bleeding, and groaning, could only excite the ridicule of the spectators. The son of Zeus in a swoon, requiring medical assistance: Who could help laughing at the sight!"

Before you conclude that the rejection of the cross is merely an ancient problem, look at the way many respond to the cross of Christ today. The Greeks still walk among us. People today still have trouble knowing what to do with it. Years ago, when I was a summer student missionary, I preached in a church in Hilo, Hawaii. As a Japanese man came out of the church door one Sunday night, he said to me: "Why must you always be talking about the suffering and death of Jesus? Why can't you talk about something pleasant in your religion?" The cross is still an offense to the modern mind. Some people have great difficulty in understanding why we hold the cross in such respect when it was the ancient method of execution. It was the hangman's noose or the electric chair of its day.

IMAGES OF THE CROSS TODAY

No, we do not know what to do with the cross today. Some have decided to sentimentalize it and sing "sweet" songs about it or make chocolate or other candy shapes of it. Others have put it around their necks, or on their lapels, or made a cross from flowers. What have we done to the cross? Goethe, the poet, reminded us to reflect again on the mystery of the cross:

There the cross stands, thickly wreathed in roses.
Who put the roses on the cross?
The wreath grows bigger, so that on every side
The harsh cross is surrounded by gentleness.[4]

But the New Testament does not speak of a rose-covered cross; it asserts the awfulness and horror of the cross. Paul is bold to declare, though, that the cross of Jesus Christ is both the power and wisdom of God. Although to some the cross might seem like a stumbling block or foolishness, God has exerted the greatest expression of his power of sacrificial love.

HOW SHOULD WE UNDERSTAND THE CROSS?

How are we to understand this cross of Christ? But understand it we must. As Jurgen Moltmann asserts, "In Christianity, the cross is the test of everything which deserves to be called Christian."[5] We have had all kinds of theories that people have tried to use to explain the mystery of this unique event. But there is no one theory, no one word, or no one image that is ever sufficient. Paul alone used many metaphors and drew his image of justification from the law courts of that day. He drew pictures about redemption and emancipation from the slave market, reconciliation from friendship, adoption from family life, ransom from the sacrificial system of that day, sanctification from their practices of worship, and the view of setting a person's account right, he got from the accounting system.

In the Gospels, there are numerous images and interpretations which the writers used to explain the mystery of what happened at the cross. There are images of sacrifice, substitution, metaphors from the law court, expiation, forensic, satisfaction, example, revelation, deliverer, representative, suffering servant, lamb, and

---

4   *Die Geheimnesse*
5   Jürgen Moltmann, *The Crucified God* (New York: Harper & Row, 1973), 7.

countless others. No one of these pictures captures the total truth about the awe and mystery of what happened at Calvary. What do we see happening at the cross?

THE CROSS REVEALS GOD'S LOVE

Notice first that the cross reveals God's love. The love of God was incarnate in Christ. The cross does not show us a God who was angry and had to be appeased but One who was willing to suffer and die to express his love. God does not try to coerce us to love him. God does not attempt to argue with us into worshipping him. God uses the persuasive power of the cross. "And I, when I am lifted up from the earth," Jesus said, "I will draw all men to myself" (John 12:32). Paul believed that when men and women were shown the cross of Christ, they would be drawn to him. God wins our love through his sacrificial love.

THE CROSS REVEALS A SUFFERING GOD

Second, the cross reveals a suffering God. God is not remote, unmoved, and impassive. God is a God of tenderness, compassion, and concern. In Hosea, Jeremiah, Isaiah, and other places in the scripture we see a picture of a God who suffers with us. God is not indifferent to our pain but takes it into his own heart. On the cross, we see God identified with us in suffering. Christ laid down his life as the Suffering Servant. At the cross, God's heartbeat of compassion has broken into our world in a way we have to see. God suffers in us, with us, and beyond us in creative holy love. With his stripes we are healed" (Isaiah 53:5). The cross reveals a self-giving and completely unselfish God. God is with us in our pain and suffering.

Every parent, who has had a child get into trouble, knows the personal agony which comes from that experience. Their action may bring shame, scandal, and sorrow. What they have done may break your heart, but as a parent, you will still love your child. Your prodigal child may fill your eyes with tears, pain your heart, burden your soul, but, even when your child abuses his or her freedom, you continue to love and support your child. Even when our sins break and bring agony to the heart of God, God suffers with us, bears us up, supports us, forgives us, and tries to lead us home again. Remember Paul's words: "For I am sure that neither death, nor life, nor angels, nor principalities, nor things present, nor things to come, nor powers, nor height, nor depth, nor anything else in all creation, will be able to separate us from the love of God in Christ Jesus our Lord" (Romans 8:38-39).

The cross of Christ reveals the redemption of God. Writing to the Corinthian Church in another place, Paul declared: "For Christ, our paschal lamb, has been sacrificed" (1 Corinthians 5:7). John the Baptist proclaimed, "Jesus as the 'lamb of God', which takes away the sin of the world" (John 1:29). In Revelation, Jesus is called the Lamb twenty-nine times. Peter speaks of our being ransomed with the "blood of Christ, like that of a lamb without blemish or spot" (1 Peter 1:19). When Philip met the Ethiopian, who was reading from Isaiah 53:7 about "a sheep led to the slaughter," the apostle preached how Jesus fulfilled this prophecy. The Gospel of John states that Jesus was crucified at the very time the Passover lamb was killed (John 19:14). "Beyond question," William Barclay notes, "the symbolism is that he (Jesus) is God's Passover lamb, sacrificed for the deliverance of God's people."[6] The writer of Hebrews describes Christ not only as the sacrifice but the high priest as well. "But when Christ appeared as a high priest ... he entered once for all into the Holy Place, taking not the blood of goats and calves but his own blood, thus securing an eternal redemption" (Hebrews 9:11- 12).

THE COSTLY NATURE OF THE ATONEMENT

Third, the cross also reveals the costly nature of atonement. Sin put Christ on the cross; not just the sins of a few persons, but the

---

6   William Barclay, *Jesus As They See Him* (New York: Harper & Row, 1962), 307.

sins of humanity. Your sins and mine, the deliberate sins of all persons, resulted in his crucifixion. The desire of all persons to be god in their own way, our self-assertiveness, our self-centeredness to be in control of the world, our god almightiness continues to separate us from God. Our sins cost Jesus Christ his death on the cross. The Apostles' Creed states that "Jesus descended into hell." Whatever the symbolism of that image means, it reflects the awful aloneness and isolation from his Father that this cross cost him. The prayer of Jesus in the Garden of Gethsemane reveals his agony as he faced the cross. "If it is possible, let this cup pass from me ... nevertheless..." (Matt. 26:39). But Jesus accepted and paid the cost. He paid, but he didn't pay an angry God. He paid in the humiliation of becoming Incarnate, in the humiliation of rejection, flogging, mocking, and death on the cross. He could not save himself and us. It cost his life to redeem us. Your sin and my sin placed him on the cross. But he willingly paid the cost. Richard Rohr states that "I do not believe there is any wrath in God whatsoever.... It's theologically impossible when God is Trinity."[7] God is not vindictive but loving.

Elaine Pagels, Professor of Religion at Princeton University, and a renowned scholar of early Christian writings, especially Gnostic Gospels, draws from one of these early writings, the *Gospel of Truth*, and notes that this author "rejects the picture of God ... as a harsh, divine judge who sent Jesus into the world 'to die for our sins.' Instead, he suggests, the loving and compassionate Father sent Jesus to find those who were lost, and to bring them back home."[8] I believe this is a valid picture of the God who loves us and seeks us out, like the good Shepherd, even in our lostness and sins.

A father and mother were waiting one night to receive a man in their home. Their son had died in wartime to save this young soldier's life. When he arrived at their house, he was very drunk.

---

7   Richard Rohr, *The Divine Dance: The Trinity and your Transformation* (New Kensington, PA: Whitaker House, 2016), 140.

8   Elaine Pagels, *Why Religion? A Personal Story* (New York: HarperCollins, 2020), 202.

They were nice to him while he was there, but when he left, the mother wept and said to her husband: "Oh, that my son should have to die for such a man." God died for sinners such as you and I. It was a costly sacrifice. Are we worthy of such cost?

THE CROSS AND THE UNIVERSAL LOVE OF GOD

Fourth, the cross reveals the way God has always related to men and women. The cross discloses the heart of God. God didn't suddenly become a loving, suffering, caring God in Jesus on the cross. He has always been the kind of God who suffers and cares. H. Wheeler Robinson's book, *The Cross in the Old Testament*, reminds us of the God who continually suffers for his people. The identification of Jesus with the Suffering Servant points to God's way of redeeming men and women. He was "the Lamb slain before the foundation of the world" (Revelation 13:8). "Jesus faithfully and courageously represented the nonviolent and loving heart of God," Brian McLaren proclaims.[9]

The death of Jesus on the cross did not reveal an isolated moment in the love of God for humanity but was a concrete disclosure in history of the eternal nature of God. Jesus did not have to persuade God to love men and women and be reconciled to them, but he revealed instead that his death was to persuade us to be reconciled to God who already loved us. In the cross of Christ, God has given us not what we deserved to receive, but grace. Do you and I really want what we think we have coming to us in life — justice? I am thankful that God does not respond to us as we deserve to be treated but loves us in spite of our sins. The cross, thank goodness, has always been God's way of relating to people. Calvary revealed the love of God which God has suffered with his people through the centuries. Molly Marshall reminds us, "Only a Trinitarian doctrine of the spirit can be sufficiently encompassing,

---

9   Brian D. McLaren, *The Great Spiritual Migration* (New York: Convergent, 2016), 92.

for it integrates the creative and redemptive work of God."[10] The God of creation is also the God of redemption whose Spirit was in the suffering on the cross.

One time a painting hung in the National Museum in Washington, D. C. where Jesus was depicted hanging on the cross. Jesus seemed to hang there isolated, rejected, and alone. But, as you study the painting more, suddenly you became aware that behind the shadows of the cross, there seems to be another figure with arms outstretched holding the cross whose face is marred with terrible agony. The artist was boldly affirming what Paul declared when he wrote: "God was in Christ reconciling the world unto himself" (2 Corinthians 5:19). The eternal God, the Creator of the universe, was present in Christ redeeming us from our sins. And God was there on Calvary, because God has always been a loving God who has wanted to redeem his wandering children.

The death of Jesus Christ on the cross reveals to us the sacrificial, loving presence of God. It is a wonder beyond our imagination. In a hymn by George Kitchin, where the tune title is called "Crucifer," the words reflect an image taken from the crucifix which the worship leader in some congregational settings would carry as he/she would march before the procession as the other worship leaders walked behind the person bearing the crucifix. They would sing together, "Lift high the cross." "Lift high the cross." This procession symbolized their desire to follow the Lord of the cross and lift that cross high. Let us seek to follow the cross of Christ as the central sign of our faith. Let us lift high the cross! Remember that at the cross we see something about God that we can never fully put into words. We bow before this mystery, and kneel humbly, and sometimes are left speechless but always we come with a sense of awe and wonder.

---

10 Molly T. Marshall, *Joining the Dance: A Theology of the Spirit* (Valley Forge, PA: Judson Press, 2003), 3.

O God, the mystery of the cross overwhelms us. We confess that we can't fully understand it. But we bow before that cross. We thank You for such love and sacrifice. May we learn to follow the Christ who loved us so. Amen.

6.

A Cry of Triumph:

It Is Finished

JOHN 19:30; 20:19-22

Fourteen hundred years ago a dramatic scene transpired at the Court of King Edwin of Northumbria. The old castle hall was ablaze with torches and a great log fire was burning in the middle of the room. The room was charged with excitement as the first Christian missionaries from Rome to visit England are sharing the Gospel story. After the first discourse is over, a hush falls on the hall.

When an opportunity to ask questions is given, a man rises: "Can this new religion, asks one, "tell anything of what happens after death? The soul of man is like a sparrow flying through this lighted hall. It enters at one door from the darkness outside, flits through the light and warmth, and passes out at the further end into the dark again. Can this new religion solve for us the mystery? What comes to us after death in the dim unknown?"

That question from centuries ago is often your question and mine. Is there any life after death? Is this world all there is? We long

to have an answer. On Easter Sunday and every other day, we seek
to know if there is an answer. Let us begin our search with our first
text from John.

WHAT DID JESUS' DEATH ON THE CROSS FINISH?

For six hours Jesus had hung upon the cross. He seemed to
realize that the end was near, and with a loud shout he cried: It
is finished!" But what was finished? The religious authorities had
finished their accusations. The political authorities had finished
their condemnation. The mob had finished their jeers and cries of
"Crucify him!" The soldiers had finished their nasty job of nailing
him to that wooden tree. Yes, these persons had finished their work.
The disciples certainly thought that their dreams and hopes of Jesus
being the Messiah and that the rule of God was at hand had been
finished by Jesus' death on the cross. Everything they had longed
for, hoped for was finished.

Remember the disciples could not easily accept the death of
Jesus on a cross much less believe in the resurrection. They were not
expecting anything of that sort. They had gathered together in a
room, most likely the same Upper Room where they met with Jesus
for the Last Supper. They were filled with despondency, despair,
defeat, darkness, and hopelessness. They were not anticipating that
Christ would be raised from the grave. They were defeated and dis-
illusioned men. They were Saturday's children who were caught on
the wrong side of Easter. They had not yet experienced the power
of the resurrection. The following lines express their dilemma:

Monday's child is fair of face;
Tuesday's child is full of grace;
Wednesday's child is loving and giving;
Thursday's child works hard for a living;
Friday's child is full of woe;
Saturday's child has far to go;
But the child that is born on the Sabbath day is brave and
bonnie and good and gay.

Saturday's child has far to go. The disciples were still Saturday's children. They were caught between the Friday of the crucifixion and the Sunday of resurrection. They were caught in the meantime. They were unbelievers. They did not anticipate the resurrection, nor did they believe it at first.

CLOSED DOORS

A Door of Understanding

Look at the disciples as they gathered in the Upper Room with their door bolted shut. They had a number of doors bolted shut, did they not? First, *their door of understanding* was bolted shut. Christ had walked among them for three years, but they had not understood what he had tried to teach them. He had told them again and again that he must die and be raised the third day. But it was not until later that they understood the meaning of these words. Their vision was limited. They did not understand, but neither do many of us. We live in the light of the resurrection, and yet there are many of us today who still do not believe. We can't quite commit ourselves to it.

False Theories about the Resurrection

Many have bought into some of the theories that are going around today about the resurrection of Jesus. One theory is that *Jesus really did not die*. Some have proposed that he just fainted on the cross. The soldiers only thought he was dead. They removed his body from the cross while he was still alive. He only seemed to have died. But tell that to the disciples who were gathered in the Upper Room. They knew he was dead. They had seen him go through an awful scourging. Many men sometimes died from that beating alone. They had seen him hanging on the cross and had seen the spear rip into his side. Even the soldiers knew that he was dead. They didn't take the time to break his leg. He was dead. It was over. They buried him in a borrowed tomb. The disciples knew that he, their master, was dead.

There are some who suggest that *the Jews stole his body* to keep the disciples from taking it and claiming that he arose. They did not want his tomb to become a shrine. Well, if the Jews had stolen the body of Jesus, they could have put an end to all the resurrection stories immediately by producing it. All they had to do was to declare: "Here is his body. He is not alive." But they never did that.

Others have said, "*The disciples stole Jesus' body.*" This would make the resurrection story, on which the Christian faith is based, a lie. A novel, *The Passover Plot,* published several years ago, plays off this theme. According to this novel, Jesus had not really died; he only swooned on the cross. He revived while in the tomb, and he and the disciples began a game of deception. Men and women might die for a delusion, but nobody is going to die for a lie. Christian history is paved with one disciple after another laying down his life for Christ. They would not be martyred for a lie which they had manufactured. Gausner, a famous Jewish scholar, rejects this theory. "That is impossible. Deliberate imposture is not the substance out of which the religions of millions of mankind are created." The existence of the church itself belies that view.

Others have said that *the resurrection was only a hallucination.* A hallucination might be possible if only individuals had had an experience with Christ. But Jesus didn't appear just to individuals. He appeared to the eleven disciples on several occasions. Then he appeared to over five hundred. That many people cannot have had a hallucination.

The disciples did not preach a lie or a hallucination, but they proclaimed an experience that they had with Christ. They didn't understand Jesus when he spoke to them about rising on the third day. After the resurrection, the blinders were removed from their eyes and they were able to realize the truth of what he had taught them.

A Door of Fear

Second, the disciples also had *the door bolted shut by fear.* They were simply afraid. They thought that the Roman and Jewish authorities who had put Jesus to death would soon come and arrest them. They were afraid that they might be beaten and crucified like Jesus. Afraid for their lives, they hid in the Upper Room. But they are not the only ones who are afraid, are they? We all have fears. The deepest fear of all is the fear of death. We are afraid that death is the end and there is nothing beyond. Some of us stay behind doors bolted shut with the fear of death, the fear of life, and the fear of so many things. We are unable to free ourselves from fear.

A Door of Despair

Third, the disciples were also behind *a door bolted shut by despair.* They had all declared that they would never forsake Jesus. Peter, "the Rock," crumbled and denied his Lord and fled. All of them had forsaken Jesus. Peter said that he would be strong; but he broke. Now in despair, after what happened to Jesus, they are broken and beaten men. They had longed for so much. They had hoped — dreamed — that this One would be the Christ, the Messiah. All of their confidence had been put in him, and now he was dead. Crucified. Everything they had hoped for had crumbled. Despair took over. They had gone days now without sleep; their spirits were all churned up, and they were empty and hopeless.

We know these kinds of feelings at times, do we not? They come upon us sometimes when we feel that we have been backed into a corner, do not know which way to turn, what to do, life has crashed in, and all hope seems to be gone. John-Paul Sartre wrote a play called *No Exit* which depicts the feelings of many today. I hear people all the time who say they have reached a place in life where there seem to be no exits. They feel trapped in a room without a door, and if there is a door, it is locked. They have come to a dead-end street in life and do not know which way to turn, where to go for help or direction, or what to do to find meaning. Life has crushed them. "Where do we turn?" they ask. "Where do we go?"

A Door of Shame

Fourth, they were also *bolted behind the door of shame*. They had fled from their Lord in his hour of need. Peter, like a whipped dog who had crawled under some porch steps, was broken with the shame of his denial of Christ. Their faces blushed with the shame of their retreat. Hiding in shame, they did not know which way to turn or where to go. Why had they not been willing to stand by Jesus in his time of need?

But we all at some time or another stand before mirrors of shame, do we not? We look into the mirrors of our mind and we see reflected things we should not have done as well as things we should have done. Our sins are by commission and omission. We are often ashamed of sins we have done and long for somebody to unlock the door of our shame to set us free. The disciples longed for more; hungered for something different; reached for something higher but at this moment had not found it.

One of my favorite writers is Loren Eiseley, an anthropologist. In his book, *The Immense Journey*, he tells about a walk he took by some frozen ponds on a cold, snowy day in Kansas. As he was walking along, he noticed a spot on a pond where the snow had blown back, and he saw a green face peering up at him. Looking down at the ice, he saw a catfish frozen in the ice, its barbels spread pathetically by its face. On a whim, he cut the fish out in an ice block and dropped it into a container to take home with him. He put the can in his basement, thinking that he would either dispose of or dissect the fish the next day.

Several hours later when he returned to his basement, he heard a stirring in the can, and he looked in. The ice had melted, and he discovered that the fish's gills were slowly laboring. The fish seemed to be looking up at him and saying, "A tank." He put the catfish in a tank, and the fish lived with him all winter. In the spring, migratory impulses rooted somewhere in his brain from a million ancestral years caused the fish to jump out of the tank as others of his kind had leaped from drying shallows to find a main channel. But his jump caused him to perish on the basement floor. He took a gamble and lost.[1]

The disciples had made a gamble and put their trust in Jesus. Now, like this catfish, they felt they were floundering on the floor like a fish out of water and the end was near. Their instincts had been to reach high for the kingdom Jesus preached about. But now it all seemed finished. They did not see the possibility of new life out of this defeat.

Easter really let the world know who was in charge. The question is whether the world is determined by the Herods, Pilates, false religious leaders, Judases, mobs, soldiers, swords, thorns, whips, nails, or crosses — force or by the love and sacrifice of God. David Buttrick says that "the resurrection is a reversal — a reversal of God and the world."[2] The resurrection is a demonstration of God's power over the world and the pseudo values of much of humanity.

THE APPEARANCE OF JESUS

Something happened, which the disciples had not expected that changed everything. Even with the door bolted shut, Jesus suddenly appeared in their midst. Bolted doors cannot keep Jesus out. Before they realized what had happened, Jesus was with them in the room. How do we explain his appearance? There is no simple explanation. Whatever else one may want to say to describe the resurrection of Christ, the Gospel writers depict it as an objective historical event. But their descriptions of this event say more than that. It is also wrapped in mystery and awe. The resurrected body of Jesus was obviously different in some way than it was before the

---

1   Loren Eiseley, *The Immense Journey* (New York: Vintage Books, 1959), 21-24.
2   David Buttrick, *The Mystery and the Passion* (Minneapolis: Fortress Press, 1992), 32.

resurrection. In his risen body Jesus was not limited by space or time. He appeared and disappeared at will. He somehow entered a room when the door was bolted shut. Earlier he had appeared to two disciples on the road to Emmaus, and they had not recognized him at first. Later he appeared to the disciples by the seashore. Although his body was different in some ways, they knew that it was Jesus, their Master. They recognized him.

The biblical accounts of the risen Christ are filled with apocalyptic and symbolic language. Although all the Gospel writers are agreed that the tomb is empty and that Jesus has been raised from the dead, they do not agree on all other details. In one, Mary is told not to touch Jesus; in another, Thomas is told to touch him. None of the Gospels give the same list of women who go to the tomb. In Mark, the sun has risen, in Matthew, it is growing light, in Luke, it is dawn, and in John, it is still dark when the women arrive at the tomb. In some of the Gospels, the stone has already been rolled back. In Matthew, an angel rolls back the stone. In some of the Gospels, it is recorded that there are young men or a man at the tomb. Some are depicted as inside the tomb, and in Matthew, one is outside the tomb, while John and Matthew write of angels.

All these accounts present different recollections which arose out of personal experiences and witnesses. The excitement of what had happened is interpreted in various ways. The writers seem to be applauding the great, unique miracle which God had done. Raymond Brown, the noted New Testament scholar, is convinced that these divergences in the Gospels are not a rejection of the historicity of the resurrected appearances of Jesus "but maybe the product of the way in which the purpose for which the stories were told and perceived."[3]

Easter sounds too good to be true, too hard to accept. It seems impossible. But it is the affirmation of the New Testament. I heard about a little girl who was being helped with her multiplication table by her grandfather. "Six times six?" he asked her. She respond-

---

3   Raymond Brown, *The Gospel According to John, XIII-XXI*
     (New York: Doubleday & Co., 1970), 971.

ed triumphantly, "Thirty-six." "Nine times nine?" "Eighty-one." And then he asked. "Thirteen times thirteen?" The little girl then scornfully replied, "There is no such thing!" But simply because she had not experienced it was no basis for assuming something does not exist. And this is certainly true for the resurrection. God did what had previously been unknown to human experience. The resurrection is a unique event.

Gerald Manley Hopkins, a Jesuit priest, once wrote: "Let God *easter* in us, be a dayspring to the dimness of us." He used Easter as a verb. Easter is a transitive verb with God as the subject and humanity as the object. Let God bring Easter alive within our hearts and minds as we experience the power of God's grace.

THE PEACE OF CHRIST

As Jesus appeared in their midst, his first words to the disciples were the typical Jewish greeting, "Shalom" — "Peace be unto you." This greeting to the ancient Jews was almost as common as our "Good Morning" today. Yet this greeting meant much more to the disciples on this occasion. The arrest, death of Jesus, and their abandonment of him had left them without peace, and they were terrified. Suddenly the Christ, whom they had forsaken and rejected, appeared among them, and they were still terrified. He calmed their fears with the familiar word, "Peace." Remember he had told them earlier: "My peace I leave with you, not as the world gives, give I unto you. My peace I give unto you."

Leslie Weatherhead tells about visiting a woman who was dying of cancer in a nursing home. When he entered the room, he said it was as though someone had lighted a beautiful lamp in the room. "You need not be troubled for me," she said. "I am not afraid of death. All that you preach is true." Knowing the probability of a painful death, she said: "I am proud to be trusted with this illness. It is giving me opportunities that I never had before." "Well, my dear," Weatherhead said to her, "you may not get better from cancer, but you have conquered cancer."[4]

Cancer may take our physical lives, as may or will other illnesses, but these ills cannot conquer us. We have the peace of the living Christ in our hearts. His peace gives us the faith and courage to know that death cannot win. We live and die in Christ.

THE DISCIPLES' RESPONSE TO THE RISEN CHRIST

The Gospel records reveal that Jesus' disciples responded in a variety of ways to the risen Christ. Their experiences were not all the same. The beloved disciple, John, responded without having to have proof. Mary Magdalene heard her name called and recognized Jesus and fell at his feet and believed. The other disciples saw him in the Upper Room, and they believed. Thomas had to touch Jesus to believe. Some other responded **to him** after the Road to Emmaus experience. Our way of responding to Christ does not have to be the same for all. Your experience with the risen Christ does not have to be like mine or your experience like somebody else's. Each of us can have a different avenue of responding to Christ. There are some persons who can never recall when they did not know God. They were brought up in church. They cannot remember a time when God was not near to them or when they did not love him. There are others whose lives are a constant wrestling match with doubt and faith, reality, and deception, evil and good. Others have an experience with Christ that is dramatic and startling. For others, their faith is simple, and it has always been easy to believe. No one experience in the New Testament becomes the example of the only way one can come to Christ. Each person commits his or her life to Christ in quiet trust and faith as she or he has experienced him as Lord today.

However, we experience the Living Lord, it will be One who has nail prints in his hands. To prove that he was indeed the Je-

---

4   Leslie D. Weatherhead, *It Happened in Palestine* (New York: Abingdon Press, n.d.), 320-321.

sus the disciples had known before his crucifixion, he instructed: "Reach out your hands and touch the gashes in my hands and side. Touch me." Nail prints speak louder than words in these moments of shock. "Look," he said. "You can see that it is I, the One who was crucified." In a similar way, he comes to us today.

Some years ago, a religious publishing house printed a bulletin for Easter Sunday which showed a healthy-looking Jesus standing before Mary Magdalene in a garden with his hands outstretched in victory. Mary Magdalene looked like a young woman and Jesus like a youthful and handsome man. But something was radically wrong with the picture. The church janitor took one look at the picture and saw the trouble immediately. "No nail holes," he said. The outstretched hands of Jesus had not been pierced.[5]

There is no resurrection without the cross. There is no crown without a cross. Resurrection was clearly linked with the cross in the proclamation of the New Testament writers. The risen Lord is the One who was crucified on a cross. There is no cross-less resurrection.

THE MISSION OF THE DISCIPLES

Notice what happens next to the disciples after they see Jesus and realize that it really is the risen Lord. He gives them a mission. "As the Father has sent me, so send I you," he declared. He had come into the world to disclose God to humanity. Now the disciples, all of those gathered in the Upper Room, are to go into the world and bear witness to what they have seen.

What do they share? They bear witness to the resurrection of Christ. They had experienced the presence of the living, risen Lord, and they are commissioned to tell this great good news to others. Because he lives, we, too, shall live. They are also to witness to the revelation of what God has done through Christ. John 3:16 gives a summary of this message. "God so loved the world that he gave his only Son that whosoever believes in him will not perish but have

---

5   Buttrick, *The Mystery and the Passion*, 29.

eternal life." They are also to witness to the redemption of God. The Church is to be the agent of reconciliation which brings other men and women to know Jesus Christ as Lord.

RECEIVING THE HOLY SPIRIT

Then John said that Jesus breathed upon them. This is not meant to be taken literally. Jesus bequeaths to them power. When Jesus said, "Receive the holy spirit," this was not "the Holy Spirit," but the power and energy from Christ as the source of life. "Receive power," he declared. "Receive inspiration." He equipped them to go into the world. Breath and the Spirit of God are often identified in the scriptures. In the creation story, God breathed on man/woman and they became living persons (Genesis 2:7). The words of the hymn, "Breathe on me, Breath of God; Fill me with life anew" catch the symbolism of Christ's action. He breathed into his disciples the breath of inspiration, the breath of the power of his peace and presence. No person can serve Christ without his presence and power in them. We are empowered by him. We are inspired by him. God is always seeking to make his presence known to us in the world. If we do not sense it, the problem lies not with God, but with us.

As we walk through the world today and lift our cups up to God, we want to be filled with God's presence. Suddenly we realize that all of life is filled with God's presence. Whenever we raise our cups under the waterfall of God's presence, our cups can never contain all of the wonder, joy, and excitement of God's being, if we are open to it. If we do not sense God in our world, the problem is not with God but with us. God is closer than breath itself. Open your life. Sense God. God is always waiting to fill your life and mine with love and joy.

When Leo Tolstoy finished his novel *War and Peace*, he did not conclude with the words "fine" — "it is finished." He put three dots. To me that is symbolic. It is symbolic that our lives do not end at death. The three dots symbolized that life goes on. Saturday is not the final word. Easter Sunday lies ahead. The disciples had not anticipated the resurrection of Jesus. If they had really believed that the resurrection was going to take place, they would have all been standing at the tomb on Sunday morning waiting impatiently for him to rise. But they had not believed it. But when it happened, they were transformed.

IT IS ACCOMPLISHED

Listen to Jesus' words of triumph again as he cried, "Tetelestai!" "It is finished!" "It is accomplished." What was finished?[6] Well, for one thing, he had *finished living life as God meant for it to be*, in perfect communion with God, his Father. He had finished *disclosing the way of the abundant life*. He had finished *revealing what the nature of God was like*, redemptive love. He had finished the *work of redemption*. His disciples understood what he meant when they declared, "He is risen!" You and I now have two thousand years of history that speak of this great event. The risen Christ can transform our lives and make us different. We need to open our lives to the Christ who comes to meet us on Easter Sunday or any day we are open to him.

THE FOUNDATION OF OUR FAITH

Paul, writing in the fifteenth chapter of First Corinthians, did not put his primary emphasis upon the teachings of Christ, as great as they are. He did not put the principal stress upon the miracles of Christ, as significant as they are. He did not put his chief emphasis on the crucifixion of Christ. The foundation of the faith which Paul underscored was the resurrection of Jesus. Paul knew that if the resurrection was not true, all the rest of the Christian faith tumbled. But the resurrection of Jesus was the beginning of the Church's hope and faith. The disciples were transformed by it, and

---

6   For further discussion of "It Is Finished" see my book *The Last Words from the Cross* (Gonzalez, FL: Energion Publications, 2013), Chapter 6, "The Triumphant Shout," 65-71.

they went into the world to preach the gospel as different men and women because of the risen Christ. His disciples were compelled to share this marvelous good news with others. The grave could not hold him. It was not the end for him. "Because he lives," they preached, "we too shall live."

Michael Green relates an incident that occurred in Czechoslovakia when the Soviet Union was still intact. A communist lecturer from Russia was brought to one of the great universities in Prague to address a gathering of students and their families about the falsehood of the resurrection of Jesus. He spoke to the crowd for a long time. When he finished his lengthy lecture denying the resurrection, an old Eastern Orthodox priest in the audience asked if he could respond to the lecture. The lecturer was caught off guard by that response but finally relented, "I will give you one minute. That's all. One minute." The priest said, "I don't need your minute. I only need five seconds." He then turned around and looked out across that enormous sea of people and suddenly cried out at the top of his voice, "Christos Anesti." The two words that begin the Eastern Orthodox Easter service are "Christos Anesti." "The Lord is risen!" At that moment, the whole crowd in the auditorium stood up as one, and there was a roar of response. "Alithos Anesti." "He is risen indeed."

On Easter Sunday our lives should be different because of the marvelous Easter story. Because Jesus is alive, we, too, have hope. Because he lives, we can live differently. We live not in despair, dejection, defeat, and in dread of death, but with hope and in anticipation of eternal life.

Death is the doorway through which we move from one house to another. It is not to be feared, because Jesus Christ has taken the sting out of death through his resurrection. We celebrate that victory today and every Sunday. I hope that your heart swells with the joy of it and that your life will pulsate with the excitement and radiance of being able to say, "He lives, and because he lives, I will live also."

Eternal God, the joy of Easter overwhelms us. We thank You for the reality of it and for what it means to our lives individually and what it has meant to the formation of Your Church. May we, like all Your disciples, continue to bear witness to this great event. Through the living Christ we pray. Amen.

The Last Words from the Cross

William Powell Tuck

CPSIA information can be obtained
at www.ICGtesting.com
Printed in the USA
FSHW011810270921
85001FS

9 781631 997815